When We Say Never

Elaine Herrin

BROADMAN PRESS
Nashville, Tennessee

To the one who dared to walk with me. . . .
your footprints are on these pages for everyone to see

Unless otherwise noted, Scripture quotations are from the King James Version of the Bible.

Scripture quotations marked (GNB) are from the *Good News Bible*, the Bible in Today's English Version. Old Testament: Copyright © American Bible Society 1976; New Testament: Copyright © American Bible Society 1966, 1971, 1976. Used by permission.

Scripture quotations marked (RSV) are from the Revised Standard Version of the Bible, copyrighted 1946, 1952, © 1971, 1973.

Library of Congress Cataloging in Publication Data

Herrin, Elaine, 1935-
  When we say never.

  1. Herrin, Elaine, 1935-   . 2. Baptists—
United States—Biography. 3. Christian life—
Baptist authors.   I. Title.
BX6495.H5A38   1985   286'.132'0924 [B]   84-23893
ISBN 0-8054-5109-9

Preface

The word *never* should never have become a part of my vocabulary. Those five letters have contradicted me many times over. Yet it has always been with unswerving confidence, boastful bravado, and cautious conviction that I have pronounced that powerful negative— NEVER.

Why is it, then, that all of that confidence, bravado, and conviction have been shaken time and again as my life has been shaped by so many "nevers"? There have been, ironically, many "happy nevers"—those that, had they not bowed to powerful and affable affirmation, it is almost frightening to think of the direction which my life might have taken.

On the other hand, there have been those nevers that marched into my life, invading daily experience with heartache, tears, disappointment, and disillusionment. Those nevers served to break me and shatter my personal and spiritual pride.

Finally, as I walk through this pilgrimage of nevers, I have met the unalterable "nevers" from the word of God. Those dependable nevers are spoken by the only One who can say with true authority, "I will never leave thee, nor forsake thee" (Heb. 13:5). Those words of promise spoken so long ago remind me that, though my own emphatic utterances may be punctuated or contradicted by failures, He is there.

This book is written at the request of many friends and acquaintances who have encouraged me to share some of my "nevers" with others who might, from time to time, know a similar sense of failure and loss of self-esteem because their nevers . . . were . . . or . . . are!

I spoke at a conference in Tennessee and shared several of the nevers of my life. One women came up to me afterwards and, with much enthusiasm, said, "You know what you ought to do? You should write these things down and put them in a book. It has helped me so much to realize that I am not alone in my 'nevers'!"

I thought about that for a long time. Then I realized that so much of what I would have to say is deeply personal, and it might be difficult for me to tell about the failures, as well as the victories, of my life.

"Put these things in a *book*?" I replied, "That is awfully sweet of you to suggest, but *I could never do that*!"

Contents

1

When I Grow Up . . .
I'll Never Marry a Preacher!

I became a Christian during my junior year in high school. As with so many teenage converts, I was spiritually inspired by and emotionally enamoured with my pastor.

During that year and the subsequent one, I became acquainted with other pastors and several ministerial students. For a short while I fantasized my future into the role of a charming, smiling, always happy, stylish, and popular pastor's wife. My own pastor's wife and others whom I came to know served as my models. While I viewed them from afar, they appeared to be such serene beings, living an idyllic life, sweetly serving beside their husbands as the traditional "help-meet."

Then I began to listen.

I listened to church members talk. I heard admiration, and I heard criticism. I saw pastors' wives given pedestal positions and then saw them victimized by chronic complaints. I watched them come, and I saw them go, the noble nomads of the cloth.

The role of a minister's wife, once sealed in a shining soap bubble of spiritual security, suddenly burst before my eyes. Always just a bit of a rebel in my own heart, I knew that there were far too many other options for a "dedicated Christian girl"—and I determined to find one.

College life in a Christian community confirmed my decision. Those late night gab sessions were filled with the chatter of hopes and dreams. We girls would all share our ambitions of love and marriage (I am a product—college-wise—of the 50s—before ERA, women's lib, and so forth. We had come to the place, however, where we as women sought professional training and looked toward something of a career. But LCM—love, courtship, and marriage—loomed larger in our minds).

I remember sitting cross-legged on my bed one night as four of us dreamed aloud. Two of my girl friends felt "called" to become preachers' wives. Betsy was struggling with piano lessons—sans any ear at all for music. Jeanie had been poring over a Greek assignment, feeling that her own personal knowledge of the biblical language would definately be an asset to her not-yet-met-but-he's-out-there-somewhere future husband. My friends spoke gently and almost piously of their intended plan for their lives. Excuse me, God's plan.

Inwardly I grimaced. Now my feelings of near antagonism toward the preacher's wife as a possible role for me intensified. The efforts of Betsy and Jeanie made my stand even stronger. For one, I did not play the piano. In fact, I was—and am—so nonmusical that it isn't funny. My stumbling efforts in that area were often the source of many a joke. In small groups, if I were singing, I would begin to get frowns; people would move away from beside me, and then occasionally someone would just ask me to "please stop singing. I think we can do it without you."

So while other erstwhile talented musicians fingered their way across the ivories toward the inevitable parsonage, I sat and drew pictures, wrote poetry, and planned my own life.

I told God just exactly what I had in mind: a fine,

dedicated Christian businessman. He would be highly successful in his chosen field, make a more-than-adequate living, and he would certainly serve in the local church. I could see it clearly: Mr. Wonderful would be wealthy, knowledgeable, teach in Sunday School, visit once a week (unless it interfered with business, of course), and people everywhere would talk about what a wonderful, dedicated Christian couple we were. Every summer we would go to a Baptist conference center. Inwardly I would beam with pride, outwardly I would glow with a quiet, well-affected expression of commitment.

Naturally such an outstanding layman would be asked to give his testimony often. He would walk to the podium with a Bible in one hand and the *Wall Street Journal* in the other. Certainly at some point he would credit me—his ever-devoted wife—for helping him achieve.

With such a fantasy of faithfulness before me, I interrupted our late night talk with a final declaration: "Well, you can throw your future to ravenous wolves and commit your family to a glorified gypsy life if you want to, but one thing is for sure—I'll NEVER marry a preacher."

As I walked down the aisle of the First Baptist Church that Saturday afternoon, I was still reeling under the overwhelming impact of the whole thing. In a matter of minutes I would become Mrs. Manget Herrin. I was marrying a preacher.

Two weeks before the wedding, the phone had rung late on Sunday afternoon. It was Manget, my fiance. (Now stop. Right here. He does attract people, but he is not a "magnet." Neither is he Man-get. The name is of French origin, pronounced "Mon-jay." If you cannot get that nasal quality comfortably, then you have my permission to say, as many friends do, Marshay. Now don't you feel better? I do!)

Manget and I had met in college. He was from Georgia, and I lived in Alabama. We became engaged and planned to marry in August. Our summer had been spent apart while we each worked at summer jobs. He generally called on weekends. Thus, it was not unusual for Manget to phone that Sunday afternoon. The message was the bell ringer.

"Honey," he began, almost stammering, "I—I don't quite know how to tell you this, but . . . well, this afternoon at five o'clock I am going to be licensed to preach." After a pause, he added the postscript, "Will you still marry me?"

I could not believe what I was hearing. Manget had been my Mr. Wonderful—the fulfillment of my dreams. He fit the part perfectly. Handsome. Intelligent. Dedicated. A great businessman. He was so good at his job, in fact, that even though he was a student working part time in a large department store, more often than not he led the entire department in sales. He was later approached by his superiors regarding managerial training. Promise of a great future in business lay before him.

I knew that Manget had taught Bible classes. He had begun several Sunday Schools while he served with the US Army and was stationed in Germany. He was occasionally asked to give devotionals and even filled a pulpit once in a while. My dream of the "dedicated Christian businessman" was evident in his life and commitment. But he was *not* going into the professional ministry.

Almost suddenly there he was, three hundred miles away, waiting expectantly on the other end of the line.

"Will you still marry me?" What could I say? (Well, first of all, "I've already mailed the invitations!")

Visions of myself stumbling through the masses of future faceless congregations flashed before my eyes. Me not playing the piano, not singing solos before the sermon. Me not wearing frothy hats, not making chicken soup.

There would be critics. But there would be encouragers. There would be suspicion, but there would be support. We would move about and leave cherished friends. But there would be new friends. We would be in school . . . and in school . . . and we would never be wealthy. We would . . .

I loved him.

"Yes," I said quietly into the phone. "I think it's wonderful. Of course, I'll still marry you." Preacher.

In the years immediately following our marriage, God taught me many things. Those lessons have served to guide and direct me into fields of fruitful service, and I wonder if I had *never* married a preacher if these insights would have come so clearly.

One profound lesson in faith and insight into the character of God was centered around His provision.

Many of the misconceptions which I held regarding marriage to a minister were quickly dispelled. However, there were several conclusions which proved not to be just stereotyped ideas—they became proven realities. (The least of those was the fact that almost from the beginning I was "called upon" to play the piano! Needless to say, many a pulpit committee chairman and missionary organization president stared in downright disbelief upon my pronouncement, "I'm sorry, but I do not play the piano.")

Among the brutal and significant realities of ministerial livelihood was the problem of financial instability and insecurity. This position was intensified for us because we were both continuing our education while establishing our home.

We attended our college classes, both worked part time in a local department store, and Manget was occasionally asked to do pulpit supply for a local pastor. To say that we were having a difficult time financially would be a gross understatement! Our money did not have to be budgeted; there was not enough to budget. Our total income was absorbed by rent, utilities, bus fare to town (for work), and the remainder (sometimes as much as ten or fifteen dollars a week) went for food.

There was one exception. We tithed. Every payday we would get home from work, empty our little yellow pay envelopes, and take out 10 percent of the wages. This Manget would place in an offering envelope and put on the mantel in the bedroom of our small upstairs apartment.

We gave our tithe, and we paid our bills. At any cost. Even when it meant skipping meals on occasion or eating gallons of dehydrated soups, cooking vessels of dried beans, and once eating fresh tomatoes which someone had given to us so frequently that Manget broke out in a rash. His neck was so sore that his shirt collars hurt—but he just loosened his tie and collar and we still ate the tomatoes!

And isn't it funny? We were happy. It actually never occurred to us that God—or anyone else, for that matter—owed us anything. We had chosen a path. The way was not easy. But we were walking, and in the face of "hard times" we were confident that everything would be all right.

At least that is how we felt most of the time.

Until the week came that the money didn't make it

from one Wednesday payday until the next. Friday night came and we had exactly enough money for bus fare to and from work on Saturday. No more. No less. But we were confident.

You see, we had heard some of our Christian friends relate such marvelous and exciting accounts of how they had strolled similar paths. On each occasion, God had miraculously delivered them at the zero hour— with a check in the mailbox. So, naturally, we knew exactly what was going to happen.

Saturday morning we were up and dressed for work. We were both aware that we had no money for the usual bowl of soup that we ate in town on Saturdays. (Weekdays we were in class all morning, went by the apartment for a quick lunch, and then caught the bus for work.) Neither of us really minded not having lunch because we knew that we would really splurge that night.

As we waited at the bus stop, and later rode into town, we talked sincerely about our faithful and won- der-working God. Neither of us voiced it aloud but—as we would later confess—both of us knowing what was going to happen. In our minds, we were doing replays of the miracles which our friends had shared with us. Only the characters were changed. This time it would be us with a mailbox miracle!

It seemed that five o'clock would never come. Finally we clocked out and boarded the bus home. Almost giggly with excitement, we dropped our last quarters into the meter and settled back to await divine deliver- ance.

The bus finally stopped at our corner. We fairly ran toward the apartment house three doors from the cor- ner. Manget was taking two steps at a time up onto the porch and flipped open the mailbox.

It was empty.

Suddenly I felt very, very sick in the pit of my stomach. My sickness began to give way to anger—hostility toward "the preacher," animosity toward some "unknown" who (obviously!) did not heed God's leading and send us that miracle check, and, finally, anger at God. He had failed.

The joy of the morning was gone. Cold and numb with disappointment, disbelief, self-pity, bitterness, and fear, I prepared a simple supper. Neither of us was really hungry. I cleared the table, washed the dishes, and went to the bedroom where I fell across the bed and cried.

Manget came in to try and comfort me. He wanted to assure me, but he lacked assurance too. As we talked and cried together, we acknowledged our own feelings of hopelessness. It was Saturday. There would be no more mail until Monday afternoon. We did not even have bus fare to get to work, and it was still three workdays until payday. We were up against a wall, and there was no way out. Faith walked out the door.

There was nothing.

Except . . .

Our eyes turned toward the mantel at the same time. There was the envelope. Set aside for our tithe was enough to see us through. Our tithe?

We talked about it. Could we? Should we? I felt "worse" and began to think that most likely I would get "worse" and would not really feel like going to church the following morning.

That was it. We agreed that we would not set the clock. We were exhausted from going to school and working. We were up at 4:30 or 5:00 every morning to study. God surely intended for us to rest. (Oh, the lines of the Bard of Avon that met my morning hours! Between daily Bible reading and Shakespeare, surely my Lord doth wist thee rest thy self upon yon sabbath morn!)

I must confess at this point that Manget was not too enthusiastic with this plan, but I was desperate enough to use my womanly wiles to convince him. We finally agreed that we would "oversleep" and use our tithe to get through the next few days. Exhausted, we went to sleep.

I opened my eyes. It was Sunday morning. My husband was lying beside me, eyes open, staring up at the ceiling. I raised up on one arm to see the clock. Disbelief! Five AM! And we were wide awake.

Apparently my devoted husband had been awake for some time. Long enough to work through Saturday night's shipwreck of faith. His vessel was back on the sea. Mine was still beached. "Stay home if you want to, Honey, but I just can't do it." He wanted me to understand, but I couldn't. "I'm going on to church," he added, "and I am going to give our tithe."

He got up, made the coffee, dressed, whistled and sang; I lay in bed and got sicker and sicker. *He's crazy. He doesn't care about me. If he did, he would not take our last penny to the church,* I bemoaned, as I silently rued the day I had married a preacher. I did not care what he did—I would *not* get up. Let him go on to church—give away our only hope. Then I would retaliate by breaking a promise we had made to each other: I would call home and ask my parents for money.

The phone rang.

I could hear Manget speak briefly and then he came to the room. "It's Mr. and Mrs. Chapman," he said, "They are leaving today for that trip to Europe and will be gone for quite a while. They asked us if we'd come down and say good-bye before we go to church."

Reluctantly, I got up and dressed. Our landlord and his wife had been very good to us. They generally did not like to have college students renting their apartment but, for some reason, had been willing to rent to us. The rent was low, the apartment nice enough, and they had made any repairs which we needed. In fact, the only problem we had ever had was when we first moved in.

Manget is tall, and the kitchen table (the only table) was so small and so low that he could not get his long legs under it without moving it from side to side. We had asked about their replacing it, but they did not. So we did. We had made our first—and only—big purchase. For five dollars down and five dollars a week, we had bought a table and four chairs. Life might be filled with many "moving experiences," but at least one of them would no longer be the table at mealtime!

I tried to cover my red, swollen eyes with a fluff of powder, but I could not hide the lack of faith that dulled my vision. We went downstairs to say good-bye.

Mr. and Mrs. Chapman greeted us warmly. "We are leaving this morning and knew you would not be here since you always go to church." I cringed. Ouch! "Yes, we were just getting ready," I lied passively.

Mrs. Chapman hastily added, "Besides, we understand that you'll be finishing up here and leaving before we return, so I don't suppose that we'll see you again."

The landlord walked over to Manget. "There is one matter of—sort of business—we wanted to talk with you about. You know that table and chairs you bought and put in the kitchen? It is so bright and cheery—that warm yellow adds a lot to the looks of the place. We were just wondering, since you'll be renting another furnished place, would you sell it to us?" Mr. Chapman took out his checkbook. "I'll pay you exactly what you paid for it, plus tax."

Ten minutes later we were upstairs, staring incredulously at a check for $49.95—plus tax. You can bet I hurriedly finished getting ready for church. Amid tears of joy, mixed with those of contrition, my own faith was riding the high seas again.

And we had learned a lesson in faith that has sustained us through many a trial through the years: Faith is not rewarded in carbon copies.

No more than God would produce Xerox Christians, would He try and deal with them in the same way. We had heard others share ways in which God had met their needs. In turn, we expected Him to act identically in our situation.

Rather than remaining open to the creative God who often surprises us in faith, we had predetermined what we thought would be His plan and His method. When we did not get that "summer rerun," we closed the door on faith.

He was there all the time, holding in His hands more than we had dared to dream. And I learned an eternal never.

He never fails.

2

I May Do a Lot of Things . . .
I'll Never Be a School Teacher!

I grew up amid a family of educators. From my earliest memories, I can recall being introduced to the teaching profession. Four of my aunts, my daddy's sisters who often filled the role of doting surrogate parents for nieces and nephews, were school teachers or educators. My mother had originally planned a teaching career, but homemaking demanded her time instead. When we children were older, she did substitute teaching to supplement the family income. My eldest first cousin became a college professor.

In my child's mind, it appeared to me that the only path open to anyone in the Jones family led to teaching. Therefore, being a bit of rebel from the time anyone can remember, I made up my mind when I was ten years old that teaching would not be in my future.

That childhood decision was reinforced in later years. Upon entering college, I wanted to major in art. But because of the added expenses, combined with a lack of encouragement in that direction, I turned to English.

That would be fine. My guidance counselor at Howard College told me what a high aptitude I had in that area; and so it was, with his encouragement, that I elected English as my major. I thought about the decision for some time. I loved to write, and journalism was certainly an area of intense interest. The professor had smiled at my conclusions and added confidently, ". . . and, of course, you can always teach."

I looked at the kind counselor levelly and coolly. "I may do a lot of things, but one thing is for certain: I will NEVER be a school teacher."

I was praying inwardly with great earnestness as I left the office of the superintendent of the board of education. I got the job! I was hired as a high-school English teacher!

After struggling with untold financial cares and problems in order to get through college, now we could make it! Seminary was ahead of us. And now the most wonderful thing had happened—God had provided for the parentheses of our lives. Our first child had been born. Now that Tim was nearly two years old, I could help with finances and assist in preparing for continuing education. True, I had always said that I would never teach; but when job hunting became my task, the most natural place for me to begin was in teaching. *After all,* I reasoned, *this is just for a short time, and for the benefits, I can take anything.*

Stepping into the position which I had previously avoided like the plague turned out to be one of the most challenging and fulfilling and satisfying things I have ever done in my entire life. Suddenly I understood all my family and friends who had devoted their lives to education. Through my own opportunities for service through the classroom, I realized the motivation behind their commitment. I also recognized the fact that I was a good teacher because of the lessons I had learned, quite incidentally, from both my family and from former teachers who had guided me through those ferocious, frustrating, formative years!

At the time I was passing naively and nonchalantly

through my classes in school, I had not realized what an important part my teachers were playing in my life. It was only as I began to teach others that I was suddenly overwhelmed with the realization that their influence had shaped me in many ways.

The second year that I taught I was asked to take one section of speech. I loved it. I had minored in speech and certainly felt qualified to handle that small class of some fifteen or twenty students who dared to strengthen their oratory prowess.

I planned my lessons well. During preplanning sessions, I had worked diligently on my four sections of English. Then I picked up my plan book for Speech I. I remembered a teacher and a class that had changed my life.

My mind went back to high school days and my own introduction to speech class. "That'll be a blast," I had told my twin sister, Eleanor. She had agreed—she had already taken the course, and she also knew what a "ham" I was at home. (In fact, we had once planned to run away and go to Hollywood where we knew for a certainty that such "darling, adorable, curly-headed girls" would immediately be "signed up" for long and illustrious careers! However, our ambitions gave way to abject failure when we decided to play paper dolls on the day of the "runaway" and forgot to run!) In any case, I just *knew* that I would *love* speech class.

I walked with the utmost confidence into Mr. Bryant's speech class that first day. We listened to endless words of admonition and preparation ad infinitum and eventually our first speech assignment was made. We were to give a three-minute speech on any subject of our choice. *Apple pie!* I thought. *When does the real stuff begin?*

Only God knows how hard I worked preparing my perfect speech. I made note cards, timed, and memorized that first oration on "The History of Motion Pictures." Each day I went to class and listened (sometimes!) to my classmates give their speeches. Then we listened to the teacher give his own critique.

But something was happening. Every day as Mr. Bryant moved alphabetically down the roll book, I watched my friends perspire and shift, and occasionally stumble pitifully through their prepared speeches. Nervousness turned to anxiety, anxiety to fear, and ultimately my fear turned to terror.

My day came. I shall never forget it. I suppose I do not want to forget it. Just minutes before time for the bell which would signal the end of class, I heard it. Mr. Bryant called my name. "Elaine."

It is still difficult to relate this exactly as it happened. The event is as blurred as my mind and my vision on that memorable afternoon.

My heart was pounding in my throat. I could hardly see where I was going. I moved to the side by the stage and somehow managed to walk to the podium. I looked down at my notes, and they all ran together. I could not read them. Was it sweat (no, not polite perspiration, stinking *sweat*!) or was it tears in my eyes? My voice was choked, my lips dry, but I tried. I announced my topic.

"We can't hear you, Elaine," Mr. Bryant called from the back of the room. "Speak up a little louder, please." I repeated the title. I was choking. The entire room began to reel. Nausea gripped me. I felt faint.

The bell rang. Class was over.

I had failed.

I had failed miserably.

All that night I relived my dismal failure and my

personal embarrassment. Fear of a repeat performance kept me awake until the wee hours of the morning.

I moved mechanically through the day, dreading the time for speech class. I would face the inevitable confrontation with Mr. Bryant. Ridicule and upbraiding from one whom I admired and had sought so to impress was more than I could handle. And above all, I had not given the speech. As usual, we would take up where we left off.

Class time came. I sat quietly, my sweat-smeared notes clutched before me, waiting. Waiting for Mr. Bryant and the familiar, "Now where are we today? Let's see."

I stiffened. I caught my breath. The pounding accelerated. The sweat. My ears were ringing.

"All right, David, I believe you are next."

David. David? I turned. Mr. Bryant was comfortably settled, his legs crossed, his grade book in his hands, his blue eyes intent on the boy going to the front.

One hour later class was over. I still could not believe it. The teacher did not call me back. He had not caused me to suffer again the ridicule or harsh pronouncements. Mr. Bryant came up to me, smiling. "Elaine, I wanted to tell you, the *subject* that you chose for your speech yesterday was *very* interesting. I hope someday you can develop it. It should prove to be quite good." And he was gone.

I do not know that I have ever loved a teacher more than I loved my speech teacher that day. Not only did he offer compassion and personal encouragement, and show profound sensitivity, but he had exercised a precious privilege: he gave me the *freedom to fail.*

My teacher *knew* that I had struggled. He recognized that at that point of my life I did all that I could possibly do. Aware of the latent potential in my life, he had given me the freedom to fail. In that brief interlude, he proved to me that success allows for failure.

That freedom to fail made me succeed. The next speech assignment was met with a good strong case of nerves (you can be sure of that), but down inside I knew that I was facing a person who cared. I was experientially aware of the fact that if I did fail again, it would not be the end of the world.

My final speech that year was an A, and following it Mr. Bryant made a little speech himself about my dismal, devastating failure on our first assignment. I went on to win an annual speech and drama gold medal in college a few years later. I succeeded because a wise teacher allowed me to fail.

That profound exercise in grace by a high-school teacher has been magnified in my spiritual experience. I believe that God, in His infinite mercy, grants us that same privilege.

Surely the divine Redeemer demands our best. At times our best efforts end in failure. During those times of spiritual strike outs, I have often been tempted to quit. I want sometimes to hide my face from the One who "sent me to the podium."

Then I remember a teacher and how he reflected the Teacher. With the same certainty of acceptance, I can try again. No longer crippled by criticism or fear of failure, but rather I find, more often than not, success. Because of the freedom to fail.

It had been with an almost cruel conviction that I had so often stated emphatically that I would NEVER be a school teacher. Yet that "never" was canceled. I spent five years before and after seminary doing what proved to be one of the exciting and enjoyable "nevers" of my life.

Every time that I looked into the eyes of my students, I tried to see them not only where they were, but for where and what they *could be*. I began to understand. I knew where that "understanding" had all begun.

Ironically, with another teacher. The teacher who taught me a lesson in faith was my own Aunt Bessie. She was my aunt, but she was also my algebra teacher. Faith? Algebra? Yes. From a master of mathematics I learned of the power of the Word of God.

Bessie (or "Miss Bessie" as she was known to her students) had her master degree from Columbia University. She had taught higher math at the University of Alabama. But her "calling" was that of algebra teacher in high school. Her reputation was hailed far and wide. Former students testify (totally unsolicited) of her firm, almost stern classroom demands and the equal care and concern she showed to all her pupils. Bessie cared not only that her students learned algebra but that they also knew God.

My aunt always went to her blackboard before Monday morning and wrote on it. Not an algebraic equation to dominate the day, but rather, in the upper right-hand corner of the blackboard, "Miss Bessie" would write a Scripture verse. The passage, which was to remain for the week, was usually a quotation from the Psalms or from the Book of Proverbs. At that time in my life, I was not especially interested in what Solomon, David, or even Jesus, for that matter, had to say. Yet, I suppose that way down deep inside, like many of my classmates, I really *did* care.

The gregarious red-haired teacher did not read the verse. She did not ask the class to repeat it. It was just there before us.

The year that I took (or I might truthfully admit, I was taken) algebra, I memorized more Scripture incidentally than I had ever done in my entire life. The Scripture stayed before us. Our eyes were riveted to the blackboard as we took turns trying to solve problems; our eyes followed the teacher as she patiently, repeatedly, worked and reworked the difficult (to me) algebra assignments.

And I have never forgotten.

"Wisdom is the principal thing; therefore get wisdom: and with all thy getting, get understanding" (Prov. 4:7).

I never wanted to teach school. I did not understand. I had changed my mind. In the midst of my own act of change, I encountered anew a fresh understanding of the One who does not change. God, in Christ, ". . . the same yesterday, and to-day, and for ever" (Heb. 13:8). *He never changes.*

But He changes me.

And I am glad.

3

It's a Shame That Happened . . .
My Children Would Never Do That!

I always felt so sorry for all those other mothers.

Whether we were gathered for a missions meeting, a social function, or were enjoying the pleasant prelude to Sunday School, inevitably someone brought up school and children and grades. That is when I would settle back with a smug look of quiet but sainted satisfaction on my face. Listening to the pathetic woes of my poor, unfortunate peers, I parceled pitying glances about me. I was glad that I never had anything to contribute in that department.

It was certainly obvious that *they* did not know how to supervise *their* children's study habits. Surely *they* did not provide a proper environment which would promote a learning situation for their children. Then, too, there was just the hard, cold fact that . . . well, some children were just a little bit . . . uh . . . *superior.*

"I am just *so* very sorry that your child is having problems. I just don't know what to tell you. You see," I would offer, fluttering my eyes, pausing, certain to gain the ear of everyone present, "My children NEVER get bad grades. They have always made all *A*s."

I did not want to sign the report card. It was embarrassing enough to have a child with a *D* in social studies. But to compound the problem, I had to face the faculty because my oldest son was in the same school where I was then teaching.

I had stared with open-mouthed disbelief at the report card. This could not happen. And the note on the report had said that unless "we see considerable improvement" Tim would get an *F* (failure) the next time around!

Never. *Not my child.* Ever since the two oldest of our three sons had been in school they had made all *A*'s. Then there came that suddenly shocking—but forgivable—day that the oldest, Tim, had made a *C.* But now the unforgivable—a *D*! And the ominous possibility—I could not even bring myself to think about it.

Where, oh where, did we go wrong? We bought books for our boys before they teethed. (They had all cut their teeth on "baby-proof" cloth-bound books, chewing and drooling delightedly all over *Peter Rabbit* and *The Little Engine that Could!*) We read stories to our toddlers day and night. They went to school in perfectly coordinated outfits and carried well-balanced, nutritious meals in their lunch kits with matching thermos bottles.

We saw to it that the boys had a record player for their room with educational records. To help the older ones, I saw to it that the baby's nap came at study time. We had followed the books and hence praised their successes and encouraged their efforts.

And now all the right and proper things faded into oblivion, and looming before me far into the night was a big, fat, ugly *D.* The more I thought about it, the larger it loomed. I was like a woman possessed.

Manget and I talked. We had hours of "conferences" just between us. In fact, we look back now with almost "holy hilarity," were it not so pathetically typical of how we Christians lose our perspective. Suddenly the most important thing in our lives became "our son's bad grade."

What should we do? We grounded Tim. He was to come in from school, go to his room, and study until supper. He could come to the table and eat with the family then go back to his room and study until bedtime. This discipline was to remain in force for two weeks or "until you pull up that grade!"

I avoided my friends. I went "late" to Sunday School. I rambled idiotically about nonsensical things like soap operas (which I never watched), and told funny, cute stories about the baby, inwardly praying that no one would dare ask me about Tim. I volunteered the latest of Jeff's marvelous second grade achievements but always went back to the antics of Jon in order to get away from any academic discussion.

Not only was I concerned about our friends and church members, but we also had our families. No way could I tell anyone in my family that my son was on the verge of failing a subject! (Isn't it funny—or sad—how life's lessons are always so plain and simple when they apply to *someone else*? A teacher had taught me the beautiful truth in giving *me* the freedom to fail on occasion; in turn, I had been able to deal tenderly and sensitively with *other people's* children in that same manner. But suddenly, this was different. Tim was *my son*. I suppose that it is like all problems. No matter how great or devastating a problem might be, the biggest one in the world is the one I face. Because it is mine.)

The inevitable came. On a Thursday afternoon my Aunt Flossie came by for a visit. While she was there, one of Tim's friends came to the door, asking if Tim might come out to play. I informed him that Tim would not be playing for a few days, and the neighbor child left. My Aunt Flossie looked at Manget and then at me. "What's wrong with Tim?" she asked.

Then I blurted it all out, tears and all. I told her how this awful and terrible thing had happened to our child! Flossie looked at me, a surprised and pained expression on her face. "And you are punishing him so severely?" she countered. There was even a hint of reprimand in her voice, and I was startled. Surely she should be as disappointed and embarrassed as we were.

My Aunt Flossie was an educator too. She had served as dean of women at Judson College; she had been assistant registrar and registrar at Peabody College and Towson State College (Maryland); she was an honorary admissions officer at West Point. In the final years of her career, she had chosen to serve as guidance counselor at the local high school. If anyone knew how to deal with scholastic problems, she would.

I looked at her almost shamefacedly. Surely she was also embarrassed and ashamed that her grandnephew was practically "blowing it" academically—and in the *sixth grade* at that!

"Oh, Elaine," she cautioned, "don't do this. You just do not know *why* a child gets a grade like this occasionally. It may well be his fault. But, again, it may not be of his own making at all.

"A child his age has so many changes to face—almost daily. You don't have any idea what his thoughts and feelings are. But one thing is for certain—he needs love, not isolation."

My aunt became stern and very serious. "I mean it. You could create a chasm between you in this situation that neither you nor Manget might bridge again. Demand reasonable study time, but do not keep on with this punishment."

My lovely aunt left. Manget and I sat and looked at

each other. Suddenly I saw myself. Oh, how ugly and repulsive. Immediately I knew where the real problem lay.

Not with Tim. My sweet, lonely, "growing-up" adolescent boy had made a bad grade. The gargantuan problem was not his academics—it was my pride!

My own selfish pride had been the root of all the misery which had resulted since report card day. *Tim* had not really, truthfully been my greatest concern. The true concern had been with my ego—what would people say? or what would they think about *me*? And those notions ruled my own judgment and actions precisely because of my own misguided judgment about other people.

Manget and I both had fallen victim to the often-fatal, always-foolish what-will-people-think syndrome. Caught up in the snares of our own egos, we were punishing our son *not* for the "bad grade," but rather, for what he had, in essence, done to us. We had to make things right. We talked to each other. We talked to God.

Then we talked to Tim.

We apologized for our own selfishness and asked him to forgive us. There was no way to undo the seven or eight days of domestic discipline we had forced upon him because of our own personal pride. But we had learned a lesson, and our own pain and divine discipline would not be easily forgotten either.

Later that afternoon I stood at the kitchen window and watched Tim—running and laughing, rolling in the grass with his dog, playing ball with his friends, loving and living every moment of a late fall evening. A while later I caught a glimpse of him sitting silently looking at the late evening sky. His eyes were filled with quiet questions, his mind with somber thoughts.

My aunt was right. I did *not* know why or what or

where! Our son was growing up and reaching out. In the light of a great big emotional world opening up to him now, maybe he didn't find memorizing all the capitals of the states to be captivating or important! Someday, in time, he would care; he would even want to know.

And maybe then we could help him. Until that time I would pledge anew a commitment I had made when Tim was born and later when Jeff came to bless our home and subsequently the same commitment with which we welcomed Jon:

"For I . . . am persuaded that he is able to keep that which I have committed unto him against that day" (2 Tim. 1:12).

We commit; God keeps.

We have committed each child to God. Through the unforgettable experience of that first trauma we have learned that when a child faces a problem, the most important thing in the world is *the child*. The problem must always be secondary, and our personal pride must never overshadow the needs of the child.

There have been many, many report cards brought to our house since that day. There have been many A's and B's, and C's. And, yes, an occasional D. And once, an F. Yes, an F.

And do you know what? We didn't fall apart. We didn't come all unglued. No one was beaten or grounded. There were some extra study hours. There was an occasional privilege withheld; there were some priorities reestablished. And along with all of those things, there was always a great deal of extra help, some "let's walk and talk" sessions; and above all, assurance that, good grades or bad, love is there.

I have talked a lot about grades, but for those of you

who are parents, you would likely agree that there are probably more NEVERS regarding our children than perhaps any other. More nevers pledged, more nevers broken!

In any case, the principles laid before us through the simplicity of an episode like "a bad grade in school" prepared us for the undoing of many "nevers" in the years to come.

I met David, a minister's son, who came to play his guitar for us. He sang softly—don't ask me what. All I was aware of was his long hair! I cringed. The son of one of my husband's colleagues sat singing gospel music with hair hanging to his shoulders. My children were products of the crew-cut generation, and I was absolutely sure that short hair was the mark of true parental dedication. I vowed that evening that none of my sons would go astray in such a style—they would NEVER have long hair.

Tim's graduation picture sits on the dresser, attired in a dark blue cap and gown, wavy "syrup'n butter" colored hair, curling on his shoulders!

My sister and her husband got a motorcycle for their son, Stephen. How could they? It was just quite obvious, much as I hated to say it about my own beloved twin sister, that they did not really love or care about their son. If they had any common sense at all, they would not have outfitted my nephew with that terribly dangerous machine! Well, we *love* our children, and they could mark it down: We would NEVER let any of our boys have a motorcycle.

Manget is a photo enthusiast. We love having pictures for our family scrapbook. Among my favorites are some terrific action shots of Jon riding his shiny new motorcycle.

*   *   *

Some of our proudly pronounced and then deftly denounced nevers have been humorous. Others quite serious and, at times, quite painful. Lessons learned through our own surprising disappointments have enabled us to minister to parents with greater problems.

Let me retract that last statement. I repeat, I am convinced that there are no "greater" problems. "My" problem, happening to "me" now, is the greatest problem. Forget any comparisons.

So we will say that no matter what the problem, God's promises and His demands are the same.

I have learned, step by step, that I must be very careful not to judge others. Too many times I have seen Matthew 7:1-2, come to pass. The judgment "with what [one] judges" is visited upon me. There is a special temptation to pass judgment upon others when we see young people getting involved in drugs, illicit sex, theft, or any number of other areas of social wrongs.

It seems that there is more erroneous or self-righteous judgment made by the Christian community than by those in, what some term, the world. That is ironic, as the Christian community should be characterized by compassion, love, and genuine forgiveness. Yet, in the instances in which I have been involved, I find that the first reaction of too many of us is to start trying to find out where the parents went wrong.

The immediate response is to blame everyone else's failures and shortcomings and wrap our robes of righteous indignation about us and say, "Well, I am so-o-o-o sorry," but inwardly we breathe a statement of calculated confidence, *It could* never *happen to my child.*

Don't be too sure. Just recently I have talked with two concerned mothers. One has a son who is awaiting trial for involuntary manslaughter. She is a Christian and has raised her son according to all the teachings

and precepts of the Baptist faith. He had a good reputation and was "the last person anyone would ever think"
would find himself in such a heartbreaking situation.
Not only did this attractive, godly woman have to deal
with the pain of her son's predicament, she was facing
condemnation rather than consolation from much of
her church community. "They are not overtly unkind,"
she lamented, "they just keep a cool distance. I need
them."

The other mother to whom I referred phoned me
recently. She is facing a problem which was once
unique but is growing in all communities. "I don't know
who to turn to or what to do," the woman pleaded. My
friend went on to say that her twenty-two-year-old
daughter had "dropped a bombshell" the night before.
She was dating regularly a young pre-med student who
was also from a very fine family. The two young people
were regular in church attendance, both good students,
and faced what the mother had dreamed and anticipat-
ed—a lifetime together. But their relationship had suddenly taken a new turn.

"Last night they told me that they would be living
together," my friend continued. "They said that they
might get married at the end of this next school year,
but are not sure. I just cannot believe that this is happening to my daughter. Please. I don't know what to
do." The distraught mother went on to say that she had
heard me speak at a conference and that I had used my
little "never say never" admonition, so that is why she
felt free to call me. "I always thought 'never.' Now it *is*.
What do I do now?"

Our children will stumble. They will err in their
growing up, just as we did (and do!). We need to state
our convictions and our position and then we must

undergird them with a love "that will not let [them] go." When they do, on occasion, take a path that leads them away, we must be certain that as they leave they know that the door is open for their return.

Whether the child is in the desert of life "wandering" or perhaps "wondering" (the latter being even more difficult to handle sometimes), keep the garden of love well-tended. (I do not have to tell you to *water* it! During those times the tears come freely.)

We have the assurance from God's Word that if we "train up a child in the way he should go, . . . when he is old, he will not depart from it" (Prov. 22:6). There have been times that I have read that and wanted to say, "Blah!" If that sounds irreverent, it is. I just had a hard time finding that phrase in the context of the verse that can be interpreted to mean, *"later on . . . he will not depart . . ."* The testimonies of many of our friends, both in the ministry and not, attest to the truth of that promise. And we have experienced it profoundly in our own family.

We will continue to say *never.* We set goals and high ideals for our precious children. But when we find ourselves grasping those nevers with tenacity, let us remember those things which the Bible teaches us in our dealings with others.

Don't judge others when problems beset them. I fear the boomerang of unjust criticism or judgment as much as I have ever feared anything. I constantly ask God to protect me from that innate desire to become His private "fruit inspector" in my world.

If you know or have a son or a daughter who has left the "garden" which has been so carefully tended and is out in the wilderness—or desert—perhaps there have been no greater words of encouragement than those

given to us by one who brought us back from our own
distant journeys:

Love never fails. (See 1 Corinthians 13.)
NEVER.

4

I Know Somebody Has to Go . . .
I'll Never Be a Missionary!

Some of the happiest days of our married life were those spent at seminary. Hours were filled with study, friendships, hard work, and challenging opportunities. Life looked good. I had moved from anticipating possible failure as a minister's wife to the point of actually enjoying my role.

Those months passed slowly at first, then so very quickly. Just over the horizon I could see the end of that seemingly "endless education" which ministerial training demanded. Manget served as associate pastor of a nearby church, attended school full time, and worked at night in a large department store. My responsibilities during those years included the care and feeding of our two children (Jon came after seminary), a job at the seminary's child-care center, and I took a few classes in my "spare time."

One day Manget came in for lunch with the most enthusiasm and excitement I had seen him exude in some time. He *always* whistles (It is a telltale characteristic of his presence most anyplace—to my chagrin, even in church sometimes!), but that day there was a veritable *concert* coming down the street! He almost ran into the apartment, talking before he could get the door closed. "The most wonderful thing has happened," he exclaimed.

"Today was Missionary Day in chapel. Honey, how I wish you had been there," he continued, bubbling with an unexplicable happiness, "A man spoke and shared the challenge of world missions. It suddenly became just clear as crystal." Manget put his arms around me, drawing me into his arena of overwhelming conviction (completely oblivious to the putrid shades of green and purple that I was turning). "Elaine, I honestly believe that God can use us as foreign missionaries!"

After the shock absorbed me, I exploded. "You are crazy! Just wait one minute—first, it was preaching. I think I handled that pretty well. And I haven't minded the little country churches where the highlight of daily experience was a trip to the one company store. In fact, I think that I am becoming a good 'pastor's wife.' But you may as well hear this now, I have *no* interest in and do not plan to even *consider* this ridiculous idea."

"But wait, please," Manget pleaded, "it isn't fair to just close you mind like that. I didn't say we *are* going to do anything." My husband smiled and added very calmly, "I just thought that, since it is an area we never really gave any consideration to, perhaps we ought to at least talk to someone and see . . ."

"No," I interrupted. I was adamant. "I do not want to talk to anyone. My mind is made up."

Manget looked down at his feet, crestfallen. He wore an expression that forewarned me before he spoke. "I've already asked him to come. He'll be here at seven o'clock tonight. Just to talk," he quickly added. I turned and was walking out of the room. "You will listen, won't you? Just for a little while?"

Of course, I would listen. I would sit ever so casually on the sofa, serve light refreshments, and smile my way sweetly through a miserable evening while my husband would ask a hundred haunting questions.

They talked. I was silent. It soon became obvious to the visiting missionary that "the wife" was not exactly doing handsprings over the idea of involvement in foreign missions. He very wisely cut his visit short. Manget and I went to bed, strangely silent.

I lay in the dark, unable to sleep. The day seemed like a dream. Or a nightmare was more like it. I needed to sleep and forget the entire episode. But in the nocturnal silence of a hot New Orleans night, sleep would not come. Visions of naked natives and grass huts danced through my mind.

I could envision my sweet children dressed in madras loin wraps, bowls of rice in their hands. I tried to see myself, but I couldn't. All I could see were white-haired little old ladies dressed in pastel flour-sack dresses, pale halos floating around their heads, being "good missionaries."

I was too human. I was unable to glide across a room with my feet six inches off the floor. I walked on a very real earth. My feet not only did not glide but they occasionally dragged through the mud. I was cut from a piece of cloth that still bore bits of bark, marking me for *real life.* Of course, God knew that.

The mental and emotional struggle ceased. I would be a commendable pastor's wife. I would even be president of the Missions group. I would lead youth missions groups. I would do anything.

Certainly, somebody had to go. But as for me, I would NEVER be a missionary.

The phone call came about five o'clock in the afternoon. Manget had come in from the church office and was in the backyard of the pastorium playing ball with Jeff and Jon. I had come in from the school where I taught and had begun supper. I dried my hands and answered the phone.

It was The Call.

"Elaine? This is Truman Smith at the Foreign Mission Board. We carried you and Manget before the committee today, and you have been approved. You will be appointed as missionaries to Guyana next month."

NEVER? Four years and a few months after that first confrontation with the idea of missions, I found myself stamping a cancellation over that sincere protest.

Many miles had been traversed. A lot of water had gone over the dam. And one of the most life-changing lessons that the Lord would ever teach me had been indelibly stamped upon my life.

You see, that issue of missions was raised again from time to time. (How in the world could any person be involved in a Southern Baptist church and *not* be continually confronted with the challenge of world missions?) I began to really look at things with more openness and honesty.

True, I did have many misconceptions about missions and missionaries. This was in part the result of having been a product of the "pre-World Mission Conference" days; also, I have to confess that I avoided going out of my way to get to know "those people" who had chosen missions as their ministry.

But ignorance and unconcern were not at the root of the issue. My biggest problem was *fear.*

That's right. Fear had characterized my life from early childhood. That fear was overt in childhood experiences with my twin sister. Eleanor and I are fraternal twins, and perhaps it was necessary that there should have been at least one major incongruity or paradox in our personality and behavioral patterns.

Eleanor seemed to never be afraid of anything. She

loved to climb to towering heights in the trees around our home. While she literally swung from limb to limb high in the treetops, I would sit on a swing suspended from the lowest limb, gently pushing to and fro, hoping my feet would always touch the ground.

When we went to the annual county fair, Eleanor wanted to ride the Ferris wheel. She'd be doubly elated if the engineer would stop the wheel with her seat on top! There she would sit, swinging the seat to and fro, surveying the entire fairground. Me? I cried when the pony went *up* on the merry-go-round!

And so we grew. Eleanor passed the stages of wanting to grow up and be "Wonder Woman" to tamer ambitions—such as a professional horse trainer! (Although my marvelous sister also outgrew that, she has never lost her love for horses.) Eleanor loved water; she wasn't a good swimmer, but not out of fear. She would ride the reckless waves in the Gulf, falling into and under the splashing surf, while I sat in the sand at the edge of the shore, bravely letting the dying waves wash over my feet.

Those childhood fears never really left me. In considering a call to missions, I found myself facing those innate fears as never before. After sorting through all of the practical and spiritual ramifications related to missions, there lay beneath the surface an insurmountable fear that was crippling any possible consideration to overseas ministry. *I was deathly afraid to fly.*

Although everyone had told me how marvelous and exhilirating it is to get on a plane and soar into the sky, I knew that the jet would be higher than the treetops and faster than a Ferris wheel! No matter how my friends, one even a psychiatrist, tried to dissuade me, I remained unmovable.

My fears were even more intensified because so often

I had found myself to be that "odd statistic." You can laugh if you want to, but perhaps someone else knows the feeling. I recall sitting with a large group of some twenty college friends in an apartment for an after-church fellowship. The hosts had a parakeet which they released to fly about the room. As the green feathered comet zoomed about over our heads, I kept darting and ducking. "Don't worry," our host said, "he *never* gets on you. He just likes to fly about." Five minutes later, guess whose hair he settled in? Right! After my perfor-mance of screaming and jumping and displaying a most unladylike show of posture, the bird was rescued (that made two of us!) and returned to his cage. Meanwhile, I kept wondering why, out of twenty people, why *me*?

Falling victim to many similar incidents, is it any wonder that I firmly believed that if ten thousand planes flew that day around the world the one that would crash would be the one *I* happened to board?

It was not just the fear of having to travel in a plane, but other fears as well that kept gnawing at me. Fear of the unknown is perhaps the greatest, and certainly in considering missions service overseas there was a great arena of unanswered questions.

However, during the months of praying and talking about the possibility of our own role in foreign missions, Manget and I came to one point of genuine agreement. We decided that if we honestly believed that "God opens doors" then conversely we should agree that "God closes doors." It was upon that simple premise that we decided to move forward, seeking mission ap-pointment.

Perhaps it appears almost simplistic, but we were, in truth, faced with a Macedonian call. Although there was certainly a reluctant commitment on my part, I would lie awake some nights expecting God to appear in a vision, and speak directly to me in a vivid "call." Well, the call did come. Not in an intangible vision in the stillness of the midnight hour, but, rather, in a most ordinary way. Visions materialized right before our eyes via the media—nameless faces across our television screens; empty eyes upon the pages of our church missions literature; challenges printed on the pages of our church bulletins. I realized that God used a different method of showing Paul a vision in his day. In our technological and electronic age, He also spoke.

The call of an omnipotent and omniscient God was before us. We would trust Him to open doors or to close them.

Well, some days that sounded good. Other days it was just too farfetched to be realistic. I suppose that down deep inside, knowing me so well, I just *knew* that the big door was going to slam shut. In fact, I guess I occasionally found myself on the other side, pushing just a little bit.

Taking the appointment procedure one step at a time, we moved from one stage to the next. Certain forms would arrive in the mail, and we were to complete them, return them, and request "the next step." I would come in from school and Manget would be ecstatic—more forms! We would sit down together on Saturday or Sunday afternoon and fill in the necessary information. I would then go to our room, and very carefully hide mine away in some "secret place." On Monday morning, after I would go to work, Manget would prepare to go to the office; then he would act out the "parable of the lost coin" and search diligently until he found my papers! With glee and anticipation, he would mail the forms and request the next step!

So on it went, step by step, moving ahead, while

inwardly I kept asking, *God, when are you going to close that door?*

Then came the turning point not only of our career but also in my relationship to God and His creation.

Manget called me at school. I knew that it had to be important because he never interrupted me when I was teaching. His voice was filled with elation and joy.

"They have called from Richmond. Dr. Charles Bryan, who is area secretary for Middle America and the Caribbean, wants to meet with us."

"Great," I responded. "When is he coming?" Several members of personnel had come to see us and interview us during various stages of the process.

"He's not coming. That's why they called," Manget went on, "Dr. Bryan is going to be in Atlanta and he wants us to meet him. I called the airport and we can leave after you get out of school tomorrow and . . ."

I could not hear the rest of it. My head was reeling, my heart was pounding, and that familiar fear was choking in my throat. Manget had made arrangements for us to fly to Atlanta. Fly. *Fly.* In a plane. In that big open sky.

Not next year. Not next month.

Tomorrow.

I would surely die.

And I did.

In the next few hours, I died to myself and to the fear that would hold me from knowing God's best. I lay in the darkness of the night hours, unable to rest. And I cried out to God, as never before, *Oh, God, I am so afraid!*

In that silent hour of genuine acknowledgment and admission of my personal fear and my total dependence upon God, He took me to the true source of peace. He led me, in my mind, to His Word. From some cloistered crevice of my mind came the words from 2 Timothy 1:7, assuring me that "God has not given us the spirit of fear; but of power, and of love, and a sound mind."

God had not given me the spirit of fear . . .

For the first time in my Christian experience, I realized that my fear was not from God. I was reminded that the only fear which He inspires is that holy "fear of God"—a reverential awe and respect for His holiness. (See Prov. 8:13 and Ps. 19:9.) Any other fear that claimed hold of my life was of satanic design. As the passage in 2 Timothy had assured me, I could face any fear in the name of Jesus Christ, countering fear with his Power, his Love, and a sound mind.

The next afternoon we boarded that small airliner for Atlanta. I could not be completely truthful if I did not admit that I was still a bit afraid. Not phobic with fear, but simply afraid. Putting one foot ahead of the other, I ascended the steps of the prop jet. Below the whirring and whining of the engines, I was silently stepping and repeating with each step, "What time I am afraid, I will trust in thee" (Ps. 56:3).

No, I did not sit by the window. I did not even look out the window! I closed my eyes as the plane taxied down the runway and lifted up into the clouds. But as the plane gained altitude and finally rose above the clouds, I responded to Manget's suggestion that I just look out. I carefully cut my eyes from the center aisle (where they had remained transfixed since lift-off) and suddenly I saw the beauty of the "spacious skies" of which I had sung since childhood. I was absolutely overwhelmed. (And I *did* sit by the window on the way back!)

That day, now so long ago, that we flew to Atlanta was only the first of many times that it would be necessary to be suspended between heaven and earth. Nor was my acute fear of flying the final fear that would invade my days. But the assurance from God's Word that His love, His power, and the gift of good sense or good judgment would counter fear, has been my companion in the face of all my fears.

I once said that I would *never* become a "real, live missionary." In June 1969, Manget and I were commissioned to serve in Georgetown, Guyana, South America. Later, amid the farewells and tears of family and friends, Tim, Jeff, and Jon led the way as we boarded the plane.

Destined for a new land, a new way of life lay ahead of us. High over the Caribbean Sea, I could not see land. I could not see the future. God had a beautiful "never": "I will never leave thee."

And I was not afraid.

5

I've Always Wanted to Paint . . .
I Guess I'll Never Be an Artist!

Life draws lines and puts us in little boxes, and we in turn fulfill society's destiny. Unless . . .

Unless the creative character is challenged by Christian commitment and we decide to "submit" ourselves to God and let Him shape and mold us.

The easy way is to climb obediently into the little box and drift drowsily through life on the waters of wishful thinking.

That is where I was. Now, don't get me wrong, I was most certainly not wasting my life in unfruitful indolence. Manget and I were finding scores of opportunities for Christian service. We had enjoyed the success of pastoral ministry in the States and then had gone on to find unbelievable joy in overseas missions service.

We had been in Guyana for about a year. I was straightening up the little sewing/storage room off the dining room when I saw it again.

Pushed back into the corner with boxes and magazines piled over and around it was the case of artist's supplies. I pulled the brown vinyl case out of the clutter. Tropic-breeding mosquitoes, strangely silent (unlike our American breed) flew out in every direction. They attacked menacingly as I disturbed the dark corners where they had sought to escape the sultry Guyana heat.

I brushed the dust and cobwebs from the case and opened it. Unopened tubes of brilliant colors lay beside unused brushes. Only the jar of thinner had evaporated. It was in almost the same condition as it had been the day I got it. The art supplies had been my "Big Surprise" one cold Christmas morning, a few years earlier.

Manget had always been a thoughtful, loving, and considerate husband. Even though we were "in the ministry," he had never tried to make me be something I was not. (Now I, myself, had made a few futile, foolish efforts, but certainly not at *his* urging or insistence!)

For as long as I can remember, I had enjoyed drawing and sketching. I had done art work from time to time in college in order to earn a little extra money. I had wanted to study art, but, as I have mentioned, turned to other things instead.

Yet my love of art had stayed with me. I made posters, drew cartoons for the school paper, designed program covers, and even had painted bold banners on canvas to proclaim forthcoming revivals! Manget had known of my love for art and the latent ambition of my life, so he had surprised me that Christmas with an easel and all the supplies that a beginning artist could need. But I never found time or money for lessons, so the paints had never been used.

After going to Guyana, I even found a need for my artistic talent in preparing line drawings for locally produced Sunday School literature.

But I never found anyone to teach me to paint.

I looked at the easel, still wrapped in its packing, lying on the floor. *I don't know why I even bothered to put these in the crate,* I mused, as I closed the art case and put it away.

A hollow emptiness settled around me. I looked out

across the flooded lowlands, across the old seawall, and then up at the bright blue Caribbean sky.

I knew it would never happen.

I would never learn to paint.

I would NEVER be an artist.

My first major art exhibit was in Georgetown, Guyana. More than two hundred persons viewed the more than twenty-five original oil paintings which represented my interpretations of Caribbean life and culture. In addition, there were religious themes reflected on canvas in abstract.

The beautiful Guyanese people gave me rave reviews, and God used the gift of art to open undreamed of opportunities for Christian witness.

Above all, I entered a doorway through one of the happiest "nevers" that it has been my privilege to enjoy.

Those paints and canvas panels lay dormant through many seasons. Then one weekend during the rainy season it happened.

Manget was gone on his regular preaching mission up the Mahaica River to a small Indian village. He had begun a Sunday School and preaching mission in that area. In order to reach the isolated community, he had to travel by river launch, and would occasionally be away for two or three days.

During the long rainy season in Guyana, when the rains come down, the floods come up! Often no piece of ground can be seen around our neighborhood when those rains come. We were literally "marooned" in our own homes.

That particular weekend, after Manget left, I found myself quite restless. The waters were high, and more rain would come. Now, the boys could not have been happier! Tim and Jeff had joined the other children in the area in "rafting" around the community. Jon, who was too young to play "The Real-life Adventures of Huck Finn," put on his father's high-top rubber boots and sloshed through the yard with his friend, Loren.

As for me, I was too old to ride the raft (it looked like such fun!), and I found no special joy in the idea of tromping through five inches of water that covered our slightly elevated yard. I *especially* found no joy in the discovery of water snakes that emerged here and there, to Jon and Loren's extreme delight!

I had read and reread my four-month-old magazines. I felt *years* ahead in Bible reading! I had written letters the evening before.

On that day, as has been the case of many others, boredom begat blessing.

Going from room to room to "straighten up a bit," I found myself in the little room.

Suddenly I was pulling out the easel; I set it up and opened the art case. I went to the utility room and poured some turpentine into an empty jam jar. I had absolutely no idea what to do next.

Grasping a paint brush in one hand, I stood before the canvas. Silently, I began to pray. *Oh, God, I can't. I don't know what to do, or how to do it. You know the images that are flashing before my mind. I can't, God, but* You can!"

And I began to paint.

To share the almost unbelievable results of those paintings would take a book in itself. The number of lives that have been touched through the creative medium of art are many.

To date I have had more than one hundred one-woman art shows. My paintings have been featured in a motion picture (*The Man Who Sang in the Dungeon*, Baptist Film Centers), on television, and in newspapers and magazines. Exhibits have been held in seventeen states and several foreign countries.

Through the ministry of art, individuals have come to know Christ; others have been challenged to greater commitment to the Lord God; stimulating dialogue with atheists, agnostics, and persons of varied religious faiths have planted seed that may someday be brought to fruition. I have become ever more keenly aware that God does not give to all of us the same gifts but that truly "Every good gift and every perfect gift *is* from above" (Jas. 1:17).

Is it any wonder that the Creator God, who splashed His cosmic canvas with myriads of color, might also use a brush to play upon the chords of hearts that stand in emptiness?

I am so grateful that God has allowed me to have even a small part in opening doors for the Christian artist. No longer is the artist relegated to the Bohemian, but new opportunities and insights into God's creative activity are making provision for the Christian artist.

And I suppose that one of the greatest lessons in faith that came my way through this experience has been awareness of that divine dynamic—that, very often, when *I* can't, *He can!*

I've always wanted to but I guess that I'll never . . . has time and again been obliterated by the yielding of self in total surrender to the creative and competent God of the universe.

More than once a latent talent or an unfulfilled ambition has been realized when God has been allowed to intervene.

For me, that is another of the avenues which keeps

the Christian life filled with freshness and vitality in my
day-to-day experience.

I was having an art exhibit in Knoxville, Tennessee,
where the First Baptist Church had sponsored my exhibition during the Dogwood Arts Festival. One afternoon when I was in a shopping mall looking for some
items, as was often the case, I found myself in the art
department of one of the stores. I almost walked right
into an elderly woman who had spent some time at my
exhibit the day before.

"Hello, Mrs. Herrin," the small, gray-haired lady
greeted me, smiling. Clutched in her hand were several
paint brushes and some tubes of oil paint. "I cannot
begin to tell you what going to your exhibit did for me,"
she almost bubbled.

In that brief encounter, my new friend related how
she "used to paint a long time ago" and had found
tremendous fulfillment in doing so. Then sadness had
come; her husband had died. After many years, she was
alone and totally unable to paint again. She had packed
up her paints and determined that "something inside
had died" and she would never paint again!

"But after going to see *Images of Love* and hearing
your testimony of how God had been the creative
source behind your paintings—well, I just suddenly
knew that I *could* paint again!" And she did.

God wants so often to change our "I can't" into His
active, affirmative, "He can!" His power pounds our
pessimism into the pavement of past disillusionments
and establishes positive achievements and possibilities.

Do not misunderstand me. I am not advocating an
"I-can-do-anything philosophy" of life; rather, I am simply acknowledging the power of the Creator God and
calling upon Christians to seek His strength and leader-

ship in at least *attempting* to accomplish that which they have longed to do.

I suppose my personal philosophy prompts this kind of urgency toward action. Ask: What have I got to lose? Nothing! And if the results are positive—look at the gain!

This method of reasoning has proved to be successful not only in dealing with matters of daily life and work but also in issues of eternal significance.

A religious skeptic was seeking advice in a certain matter. He said that he knew that we Christians prayed and sought answers from our God. In his particular predicament, he had exhausted all human resources and had come "to the end of his rope," as he put it.

"Then why not ask God?" I suggested.

"But you know that I do not really believe in all that; besides, if there is a God and He does hear and answer prayer, what if He says no to me?" my friend queried.

"If He says no, you don't have it anyway, so what have you lost?" I smiled, knowing my God, "And, then, if He does say yes, you will have gained two things," I added, confidently.

"Two?"

"Yes. You will have what you have asked for, and you will have to acknowledge that God *is* and that He *does* —you'll have a new faith!"

Together we prayed. Where all else had failed, God provided the needs of the young man. His "I can't" became "He can!"

The desires and wishes of our hearts are not always so spiritual or deeply involved. Often they revolve around the ordinary routines of daily living. However, I have found that God's intervention and strength in the seemingly mundane or normal day-to-day experiences of life are what transform *existence* into *living*.

Have you ever taken a highly complicated recipe and wished that you could produce the culinary master-piece shown in the accompanying photograph? After looking at the picture, reading the recipe, and reread-ing the instructions, have you tossed it aside with a sigh of defeatism and turned back to "old faithful"? Too often one resigns, "I could never do that! It would be a total flop."

Shirley was like that. She loved to cook and especially to bake. Her family—a husband, two robust, nearly grown sons, and an adolescent daughter—all attested to their mother's outstanding ability in the kitchen.

Living in a small community where there was no bakery, Shirley was called upon from time to time to "make a little cake" for some special occasion. That was the limit of her horizon.

But as time went by, Shirley began to look at pictures of lovely decorated cakes; in her own mind, she began to have creative ideas about "special occasion" cakes. But she had no idea about *how* to do it.

Shirley is a committed Christian. She led the Baptist Women's group in her church. It may have seemed strange to outsiders, but at a prayer session Shirley shared a unique request: She felt that God was going to use her to help with the family income at home. Her idea was to bake nice cakes "and fix them up in lovely and unusual ways." So she asked the women to pray with her that God would show her and teach her what to do.

He did. Her little "bakery at home" became a thriv-ing business. She came up with ideas none of us had ever seen in books. Her source of creativity had been the Creator, and even her bakery products showed it. Her colors were purer, her designs sharper, her delicate flowers were finer. God was her teacher, and Shirley's "I can't" became "He can."

If you are reading this and think that the idea of baking a cake becoming a spiritual exercise is somewhat strange, consider this: God taught me to *swim!*

There is no doubt in my mind whatsoever that God did it. I have related earlier my intense fear of water. One of my earliest dreams, which I recollect, was a "bad dream" which centered around water. When I was four years old, we moved to my father's old farm place in south Alabama and lived there two years. A creek ran through the pasture, and we children were repeatedly warned to be careful around it. That sober admonition is likely what prompted my nightmare. In any case, in the dream I was to try to jump across the creek. My sister, Eleanor, jumped first, and (of course) she made it. She called to me to follow, and I jumped. I didn't make it. The frightening dream framed in my sleep pictured me, spread-eagle, lying on the bottom of the creek.

Pseudopsychologist that I tend to be, I always carried that dream, and it recurred from time to time. Also a bit of a mystic, I would wonder if it were meant to be some kind of warning. Whatever the position, I viewed it as some sort of ominous sign and associated deep water—*any* water—with a dire threat to my own life.

One of the most frightening experiences of my high school years was when I was lounging poolside with friends and one of the athletic boys was going about picking up girls and throwing them into the pool. I was quite surprised when James picked me up and tossed me into the deep end of the pool. I screamed and sputtered and bobbed, flailing arms and legs frantically. As I went back under, Eleanor shouted that I could not swim. I was rescued, and the show-off apologized profusely. My fear of drowning intensified.

But I never learned to swim.

Years passed, and we were living in Guyana (which, ironically, is an Amerindian word meaning "land of many waters"). Bordered on one side by the muddy Atlantic, the tropical South American countryside is crossed by canals and cool, dark creeks which travel through dense jungles. Many of the villages and areas are accessible only by boat—*karias* (canoes) or river launches.

It was into one of those quiet river inlet villages that the boys and I were going along with Manget to visit a mission church. The old river launch looked right out of *The African Queen*, and the old Hindu pilot/captain/guide welcomed our family aboard as his only crew for that particular trip.

I felt a bit tense, but even more "dramatic," as we chugged lazily down the river. Alligators rested on the banks, blinking indolently in the hot sun. They blended into the marshy, mudbank surroundings and were almost indistinguishable until they slid idly off the banks into the water. Parrots flew through the treetops, and other tropical birds provided a cadence to our trip.

We stopped at the mission at Grass Hook, visited with Chamwattie and some of the children, then, back on the launch, we headed toward Biaboo.

Suddenly the monotonous murmur of the engine was interrupted by a noticably irregular coughing and knocking; then with one weak groan, the engine died. Our pilot clanked, chinked, clanged, pulled, looked, and finally said in his peculiar pidgin English, "De boat broken. I be back." From seemingly out of nowhere a man in a small *karia* appeared and just as quickly our "guide" was over the side of the launch, and away they went.

We all stared at the little tree trunk canoe as it went around the bend in the river and disappeared—carrying our pilot/captain/guide with it. Then we stared at each other in disbelief. Without a word of explanation as to where or when or who or what, we were left adrift on the jungle river. Slowly and quietly, our launch drifted with the tide.

Suddenly, with our guide's departure, the picture-book alligators loomed menacing and frightening. As the launch drifted to one side of the river, two young children appeared in a small clearing by the bank. Black Indian eyes shone brightly. A shy girl with her fingers in her mouth looked at us with puzzled apprehension—we were likely the first white people she had ever encountered. The dark boy, younger but more gregarious, called out to us. "I tie you now!" He scrambled to the water's edge and caught a rope from the stern. Quickly and adeptly he tied it around the trunk of a sloping palm tree. Then the two youngsters backed into the clearing, squatted on the ground, and watched us in wide-eyed silence.

I cried.

That was not the first nor the last time that I would look around at strange or alien surroundings and question my own spiritual sanity with, *What in the world am I doing here?* Now my bewilderment was coupled with a growing fear. What if we were left here forever? What would we do? Where is the man? It's getting late—what if it gets dark?

Manget examined the engine. He knew nothing about it. He gazed up and down the river in vain for sight of another boat or another person. Anyone. But we were alone, except for alligators, birds, piranha (voracious freshwater fish that attack any animal—even people!), and two curious children crouching in the bushes!

In the midst of all of this, Manget was trying to calm and encourage the children. Assuring them that this was another "adventure" to remember, that everything was going to be fine, he began to make something of a game out of the whole situation. It wasn't easy. Not with me crying and sniffling and making all sorts of evil pronouncements and prophesying the direst of consequences upon our river outing.

Finally I got myself together, with the help of a loving husband who reminded me that nowhere in the whole world did children "just happen," so, if there were children near us, there would surely be other people living back up in the jungle. If nothing else, he would go in there and seek help.

I stood on the launch and looked at the water below. I thought of all the children who had jumped into the river and had swum around our boat when we had stopped at Grass Hook. ("There's no 'pee-rhy'—their colloquialism for piranha—right here," they had assured us!) I reconsidered their happiness and laughter, and the joie de vivre which they expressed, even though they spent their lives in the remote river village.

I compared the simplicity of the river people with my own life. I thought of the importance I placed upon the luxuries I enjoyed and the opportunities which life had afforded me. And, for some strange reason, I admitted my personal envy that these beautiful river people could jump and splash about and swim—carefree and lighthearted. With all "my worldly goods," I had never learned to swim!

From somewhere out of the recesses of my mind, I

suddenly made a decision. I really *wanted* to learn to swim! There I stood, thirty-six years old, looking at the bright skies reflected in the river, and I made something of a promise to God: "Lord, you are going to get us out of here. I know that. I do not know all the purpose in our being stranded here for these hours. But I do know one thing: With your help, when I return home, *I am going to learn to swim.*"

We got out.

As quickly and almost as mysteriously as our boat pilot had disappeared, he was back. He jumped from the canoe onto the launch, stuck something onto the motor, picked up a pipe and whacked the engine with one heavy blow, and immediately it started. We went on to Biaboo and back home.

And I learned to swim.

Past the opportunity of cool, green Gulf waters; miles away from luxury swimming pools; years beyond college gym pools, I made my first swimming strokes, staying afloat, in the dark, black waters of a jungle creek.

Colored by the tannic acid that washes through the mountainous jungles, the almost tea or coffee-colored water of the creeks is clean and icy cold. In one such creek at Manari Ranch on the Rupununi River, I prayed inwardly, "God, I am so afraid. Everytime I have ever tried, *I go under!* I can't. But I know that *You* can." And as I rested myself in His care, amazingly, for the first time ever, I did not sink when I tried to swim!

Later I polished and practiced my swimming at Dakara Creek where our mission family went for outings on those rare but wonderful occasions. Never again would I have to just sit and watch others enjoy the creek or the pool or the ocean.

Little did I know that God was preparing me for Grenada. We would later leave Guyana and plant our lives on a tiny Caribbean island, where the *only* thing we could do for recreation was go down and "take a swim."

I thought I would *never* be an artist; I am. I believed that I would *never* learn to swim; I did. List my own countless "nevers" along with those of so many others who have learned that life may not "begin at forty" but, regardless of one's age, life begins at *faith*.

The God of our nevers wants to change so many of our "I can'ts" into His assuring "He can."

The God of our nevers is ever with us.

Forever.

6

They Can Do That . . .
I'll Never Send My Child
Away to School!

We made the long, hot trip to the airport with our co-workers. Within four years we had watched three different couples who labored with us in overseas mission service as they put some of their children on a plane and sent them to the States to complete high school.

After one such episode, we were driving home in the brilliant sunshine, the air made steamy by itermittent showers. There being no such "animal" as an air-conditioned auto in the tropics, all the car windows were open and the breeze was blowing the sweat off our faces (and our hair into our eyes!).

"How could they do it?" I asked Manget. He was as visibly moved and disturbed as I was. We were both feeling the hurt of the separation. You see, Mission families are strange units. Matched together by an objective Board, individuals from a variety of backgrounds with sometimes potentially opposing personalities, are wedded together in ministry. A somewhat mystical union joins them and as a result they weep and rejoice with each other. (Does that sound strangely familiar?)

And so we had wept with our friends in their hour of great hurt. But all the while, we had both violently disagreed with their decision.

Manget and I had faced the often troublesome problem of education for our children before we left to go abroad. Knowing that we would be in an area where there was generally inferior quality in education, and often tremendous difficulty in getting expatriates into local schools, we made our firm and unquestionable decision: At no time, prior to college, would we ever send a child back. We might resign; we could possibly take a leave of absence; but absolutely, unequivocally, positively, we would not be deterred from our decision.

"I don't know how anyone who really loves and cares for their children could do that," Manget responded, as we continued our journey home. He obviously sensed my grief over the idea of such happening to our family. He reached over and took my hand.

"We won't do it, will we?" I sought reassurance.

"Of course not," he nodded.

I relaxed.

That may be what other people chose to do, but for us the matter was reaffirmed and settled. We would NEVER send a child back for high school.

The day Jeff left to go to the States to finish high school will never be erased from my mind.

Manget and I had our cry in each other's arms the night before. We could not let our tears mar the joy of the journey for Jeff. He was deliriously happy to be "going away to school."

We had been transferred to the island of Grenada where we had initiated Southern Baptist mission work. The tiny tropical island was not only a haven for yachts as they sailed the emerald waters of the Caribbean; the isle of spice had been a haven of happiness for the Herrins.

From the very first day of our arrival, when the

manager of the local Holiday Inn invited me to have an art exhibition for hotel guests, we had seen God at work in miraculous ways.

Manget had developed a prison ministry, perhaps unlike any of its kind anywhere at that time. Our church began and flourished. Our boys loved to roam the hills, comb the beaches, and quickly became experts at snorkeling and sailing. Their sea aquarium sported spectacular tropical fish, and hours were spent in observing the beauty of sea life.

And, of course, they went to school.

Jeff had always been an exceptional student, but we did not realize *how* exceptional until the end of his junior year (the eleventh grade) was approaching.

He came in from school one day, and we sat on the veranda. I was tutoring him in French by correspondence to supplement his local studies. (Who was tutoring whom?)

"Mom," he said, "the headmaster told me today that I can graduate this year if I go ahead and get my senior English done." The boys were in a mission school which was operated by an independent mission group. The program was basically self-study, and Jeff had breezed through at his own pace. "I don't really want to finish this year," my son continued, "since I am only sixteen. But then, I won't have anything to do next year. They did say that I might begin some college work by correspondence."

Somewhere between *ouvrez la fenetre* and *fermez la porte,* my heart nearly stopped. *Change the direction of this conversation,* my mind shouted.

"That's great," I eagerly pushed on, "then you'll be ahead when you go back for college." I picked up another vocabulary card and tried to pretend the conversation had never begun.

A few days later Jeff was back on the subject. He has always been able to drop very crucial events—bombshells—with such nonchalant aplomb that we are never really sure what happened.

"I was just thinking," he began. "Do you realize that when I go back to the States for college, I will never have ever had even one year in a real American high school?"

Manget and I looked at each other. How do you argue with that? You don't. You think. You pray. You cry.

We had to make a decision—a decision that we had not had to make with our oldest child. We had been fortunate enough that our regular furlough coincided with our oldest son's senior year in high school. So we had been there to see Tim through that year stateside.

Admittedly, leaving Tim behind to begin college at Samford University in Birmingham, Alabama, when we returned to the field had been difficult; saying good-bye to a college freshman was painful enough. But, then, we were in great company in that parting, as Tim joined hundreds of other freshmen.

But the idea of sending a sixteen-year-old back to the States to finish high school was—until now—unthinkable. An hour of decision had to be faced.

What would we do? We were in a new mission field. There was no other missionary in the field of church development. We had all new converts, all young Christians. No national was in a position to take over the work. A tremendous investment had been made in initiating the work, and a stewardship investment was there.

We also had a son. We had an obligation to him. Without asking, he had asked to go away. Jeff had a good mind; he was being deprived of taking part in any scholastic competition and expression of academic achievement among his American peers.

Suddenly the harsh judgment which I had passed upon my colleagues in years past came ringing in my ears. I had shared their tears, but only now was I beginning to share the real reason for those tears. The agony of one of the most painful and heartrending decisions that we—or anyone, for that matter—would ever make was upon us.

We would send Jeff to the States to complete high school. We were face to face with one of life's hardest hours—separation from someone dearly loved.

During those grief hours before Jeff left, we shared his eagerness and planned with him with outward enthusiasm. I am confident that he saw the pain behind our plastic smiles. We certainly saw his.

I kept telling myself, *I can't live through this. I just can't.* I kept crying out to God, "Where is Your grace?" At one point I literally shouted at Him, "You promised it, God, now where is it? God? Please!!"

And then, the night before Jeff was to leave, the most amazing thing happened.

Peace. An inexplicable, calm, beautifully quiet peace settled in and around me. Tears? Oh, yes! We all sat together in the living room. On the bay below the house, the surf was gently pounding. We talked of the future, praised Jeff for his accomplishments (he had been granted a full-tuition academic scholarship to one of the leading prep schools in the Southeast); then we prayed together and went to bed.

For what would be the last time in many, many months, I stopped by the doorway and said, "Sleep sweet," and heard Jeff's usual response as he turned toward his brother's bed and laughingly said, "Good night, Jon-boy!"

The subsequent peace and inner joy which sustained us in such a painful time of separation could possibly be explained by an illustration from a well-known book. In the account of her early life, Corrie ten Boom, in *The Hiding Place*, relates a particularly difficult time in her young life. She was facing the reality of that final separation that death would eventually bring to her loved ones.

"Father sat down on the edge of the narrow bed. 'Corrie,' he began gently, 'when you and I go to Amsterdam—when do I give you the ticket?'

" '. . . Why, just before we get on the train.'

'Exactly. And our wise Father in heaven knows when we're going to need things, too. . . . When the time comes . . . you will look into your heart and find the strength you need—just in time.' "

For Manget and me, that was sufficient explanation. I kept waiting for that grace. It did not come in the days preceding; but in God's own time, he gave us "the ticket" when it was time to get on the train!

We had done it again. Perhaps I, more strongly than any, had said, never; but we did. Under God's leadership our selfish never was relinquished to His glorious always.

The result of our decision served to affirm that we had truly acted under God's guidance. Jeff graduated from Darlington High School in Rome, Georgia, that following spring. I was privileged to be present as he received the senior award in math, the senior award in English, and the school's annual award in creative writing. I swelled with justifiable parental pride and offered an inner prayer of gratitude as his academic scholarship to Davidson College (North Carolina) was announced.

Admittedly, the initial separation had been very

painful, but the end result of our own inner hurt had more than adequately justified our decision.

Separation is one of those facts of life that everyone must face in some form. Whether it be the case, as was ours in this instance, of sending a child thousands of miles away to school or off to college in the home state or the bidding good-bye to a youth who goes to serve his country or moving away from a familiar home, the pain is no less, the sense of loss as certain. Surpassed only by the grief-pain of final separation in death, the temporal good-bye to those we love hurts deeply.

Surely you have experienced this in any number of ways.

The moving van packs the last box, closes its doors, and moves away, while your dearest friends put the last piece of luggage in the car, turn tear-stained cheeks to your own, and your best friends are gone. The familiar words across the hedge, the "always there" friend upon whom you've depended for years, the laughter and tears and "street-talk" which you savored together— it's all over. A friendship shared and treasured becomes a memory.

The child who cried as an infant, who ambled and scrambled as a toddler, recited and sang as a preschooler, played, memorized, and cried through early school days and adolescence, who suddenly "grew up" one summer and became not only your child but your friend—has gone away. The bedroom is strangely silent; no one needs to "borrow the car" or "wash this for me, will you, please?" An unpleasant emptiness settles in. Oh, yes, they come back. Back for a holiday; spring break; an occasional vacation. Back. But not really *home.*

For home is that place in some nebulous future out there, beckoning the young adult to his or her own

unique establishment. "Home" as we know it, and as
our children will know it, is in the heart.

Home is that assemblage of feelings, memories, ambitions, and faded dreams that remain with us always. I
suppose that is why so many parents, in their accelerated ambitions to provide a story-book environment for
their children, have so often missed the mark. In
stretching themselves beyond their means to provide
things, they are giving their offspring few memories—
and fewer dreams.

We need memories. And we need dreams. That is the
"stuff" that helps sustain us when separation comes.
Without dreams and memories, faith and hope lie buried in uncultivated regions of our hearts. With them,
we recognize another of the paradoxes of the Christian
faith: Separation sometimes brings us closer together.

We found this to be true in our own experience.
Being separated, first of all from our own families as we
went abroad, and later from our children as they were
away at school, brought us closer together than we had
ever been before!

Surely we had prayed for our children from before
their births. But much of our prayer, through the years,
had become rote. When they went away, we embarked
upon an experience of intercession such as we had
never known. This was true of our immediate families
also.

Our children and other family members had a similar
experience. They wrote in letters those things they
couldn't seem to say face to face (or perhaps felt no
need to say them before). Through this extended relationship, we came to know each other better, to understand one another more fully, and, if it were possible,
to love each other more.

I do not believe it is by chance that, even as I prepare this chapter of my manuscript, I have just lived through one of life's most difficult days— that final separation which we on earth experience.

Monday morning, five days ago, my father died.

Here I am, thousands of miles away, on a tropical island, and the phone goes cold in my hand as my sister, Eleanor, says, "Daddy's gone."

Another hour of separation, which I was certain that I could not face, has come. A hurt that is beyond definition invades my total being. My sublime and sometimes quiet faith yields to an outburst of my very human emotions. I cried. I even yelled. "Daddies aren't supposed to die!" I cried out, "Not mine, anyway!"

A kind and well-meaning Christian friend came to comfort me. "Don't cry," she said, "you must trust God and not weep. He's passed on to a better place."

I looked her straight in the eye and said, "No! My father *died*. He is *not* 'gone on'; he has not 'passed away'; he did not 'cross over Jordan.' My father *lived* —he lived life boldly and fully. And now he has *died*. That is a fact, and soft words can't change that fact."

I wept, and I cite Jesus as my example. The Son of God felt acutely the pain of that inevitable separation when his friend Lazarus died. The divine God in flesh was not ashamed to show the emotion that spilled over into hot tears. Jesus wept for the loss of his friend; Mary and Martha cried for the loss of a brother.

I wept for the loss of my father.

But even in the midst of an overwhelming grief, as the merciful Father of heaven allowed me to express my hurt, and my loss, I found again that God's grace *is* sufficient. He let the memories of childhood and subsequent memories of the final days at home before returning to the mission field assuage my grief. He reminded me of that last day, as we were leaving, when Daddy took me by the hand and looked directly into my eyes and said, "I'm going to be seeing you, you know."

My father was already sick. But he knew he could have weeks, or months, or even years. Deep in his heart, however, I believe he knew that he would not see us again in this life. But he had that assurance which only God's people have, that even the separation which death brings is not the final word for the family of God.

Death does bring down a permanent curtain in this life. Other separations are equally painful at times, but not equally permanent. However, this does not make them any easier to bear.

In remembering the pain in our hearts in sending Jeff away to school, I have to consider the equally difficult pain my own parents must have felt as they watched us—time and again—board a plane and leave. I am reminded of the literal grief I experienced as a teenager when my best friend moved away. There comes to mind, even more recently, the profound display of emotion shown by a small boy when we left for our last furlough to spend a year in the States. Marcus had no family to love and care for him; he came to church for almost every service and usually sat with me, sang with me, and talked with me about school.

The night of the church's traditional farewell for us, the child went to pieces. He sat clutching me, his face buried in my lap, heaving and choking and struggling with tears of grief. Someone he had grown to love was going away.

Is it any wonder that when we are sometimes given a *choice*—an opportunity to avoid, even momentarily, the pain of separation—that we shout, "Never"?

The day that our prideful *never* bowed to God's direction, we did not know what great store awaited Jeff in his continuing education. It causes me to wonder how many people who vow, "I'll NEVER leave this church . . ." or "I'll NEVER let my firm transfer me . . ." or "I'll NEVER . . ." are, themselves, missing out on God's great storehouse of surprising provision.

Manget and I are grateful that prejudices and our own selfish needs did not bind us to a *never* decision made so long ago. We learned anew that God's ways "are above our ways" and that each situation must be treated with deliberation, prayer, and openness to God's directives. When His direction and leadership bruises us and leaves us looking up in times of life's lonely hours, He is there to remind us that He will not leave us comfortless.

Never.

7

I Surely Am Sorry That Happened to Her . . .
You Can Be Sure I'll Never Be Tempted!

It was all so sad. We sat at our ladies' meeting and "prayerfully discussed" Myra and the terrible situation that she had gotten herself into. It was so very clear. There were most definite conclusions that our godly group gleaned from the facts that lay before us.

Our dear friend certainly must not have ever been *really* saved. Well . . . if she was, it was now a fact that she was terribly backslidden and far from God.

Then, too, some of us were confident that she had most likely been "fooling around" for a long time, and now she had finally been caught!

The list began to grow, ad infinitum. The more we talked and shared our "Christian concern," the more juicy details we gleaned from those present who knew from "very reliable sources" just exactly what had happened.

I listened. I participated—not actually with many verbal contributions, but with sad-eyed, somber nods, and occasionally offering a weak, unwelcome word that, "Yes, that is really too bad. We should pray for her."

Myra had not been a close friend, but she was an acquaintance whom I had admired. A warm, affable person with a unique ability to teach the Bible. Her Sunday School class had grown steadily, and her apparently genuine concern and compassion for others was no small reason for the faithfulness of the members of her adult class.

With two children and a fine husband, Myra and her family looked to be the ideal family—an old *Saturday Evening Post* cover translated into life. I had not come to know her well; but what I did know, I liked.

So I was as stunned and shocked as everyone else when news came that Myra's marriage was in trouble. To top it all, rumor had it that she had become quite involved with a deacon in the church.

What happened to her and why, I did not understand, but as we continued to delve into the whole sordid episode, I knew one thing: I would NEVER fall into such temptation!

How on God's good earth could I have *ever* gotten myself into such a dilemma? How could what began as a perfectly innocent and meaningful relationship have evolved into one of the most turbulent times of temptation I had ever experienced?

Questions pounded against my brain: Am I genuinely, *really* a Christian? Of course! Have I slidden "away from God"? No, I was not in a backslidden condition—in fact, the whole thing began when I was working on Bible study materials and was seeking to help him with some related Bible teaching!

He was a family friend. We all cared so much. Then I had found myself caring too much. I sensed the potential explosion coming, and I was struggling with my own passions, my Christian convictions, and my love and commitment to the man I had married.

I did not know where to turn. Frantically I tore through the books in Manget's study. (He was so proud of my renewed enthusiasm in theological matters!) I read life stories, biographies of great saints, past and present. I poured over word studies; I delved into commentaries. At this point, I suppose I became most disillusioned and went through some of the most painful times of doubt and despair.

Every writer whom I came across included sections where they discussed "quite frankly" their shortcomings—sins that troubled them. "Aha!" I would exclaim inwardly, hoping to find through their confessions help for my own infirmity. So I would read on in hopeless despair: failure to read the Bible. (Dear, dear God! I was soaking Scripture like a sponge, trying to find God's answer to *how*. I knew *what;* I needed to know how to escape the temptation that was before me!) Writers lamented of times when they became too busy to pray. (Help! I had become a literal perennial pray-er—petition incarnate, moving through every hour of the day praying for wisdom, power, and deliverance.) The sainted sages of my husband's library, and in the books which I purchased for myself (book stores benefitted from my temptation) seemed to relegate my own particular temptation to the forests of never-never land.

Well, why should I blame them? That was exactly what I had done. Until the fires of temptation began to fan me toward personal infidelity, I had vowed that such a thing did not happen to "real Christians" and certainly would *never* happen to me!

It became obvious that I was not going to find the answers in books at that time. I think that it is for this very reason that Manget and I agree that this chapter should be included here. Because there are readers now who are already shocked. I can almost hear you clicking your tongues in disgust, pronouncing upon me that same judgment which I so often passed upon others.

Well, you can stop raising your eyebrows. I'll answer those questions for you: Yes, I was a Christian. Yes, I was walking close to God. Yes, I was seeking God's deliverance from an emotional involvement that was on the verge of becoming physical.

No, it was not easy. There was no magic formula or Scripture verse to quote and "make it go away." It hurt. It hurt me, it hurt my husband, and it hurt my friend.

And together we found some answers.

First of all, I learned the value and worth of a wonderful husband. The writer of Proverbs wrote of the worth of a good woman, but I would like to acknowledge the worth of a good man!

I believe that the fact that I did come out of the valley of temptation unscathed must be attributed to Manget's love and understanding. He did not reject me; he rescued me.

Together we began to look at our own values and concepts regarding love and marriage. We found some faults in the background of traditional teachings in this area.

One thing that helped me tremendously and set me free from unwarranted feelings of guilt was related to past instruction regarding love. I was taught after I became a Christian that "out there, somewhere, God has that perfect person He has chosen just for you to love." I was encouraged to seek, prayerfully, that person; and I did. I found Manget, and he found me.

According to that "divine design" about which we had both been taught, I had found the only person whom I would ever love, and therefore I would never love anyone else. With that concept, I was totally unprepared for what lay ahead.

I began having inner struggles, for when God's love

invaded my life, I found that, deep inside, I loved many, many persons. Now, I did not just "love them in the Lord," I *loved* them. I actually, humanly, love people very easily. *But I was not supposed to.* So I would suppress that genuine emotion—that love—and I would "play Christian" with my feelings, and deny any real, honest feelings of love. Therefore, because I would not ever acknowledge my true feelings, I could not sublimate them in satisfying, meaningful ways.

Then the inevitable happened. All of those pent-up emotions came to a head and were on the verge of explosion. And I was turning in desperation to God for understanding and power.

To say that one will "never love but one person" may be all right for some, but there are others of us who do not operate that way. Loving other people is well and good in itself. *Finding acceptable expressions of that love is the key to right Christian thinking and living.*

What, then, does that kind of attitude do to marriage? you may be asking. It elevates it! It is one thing if Manget says to me, "I love you. You are the only person I have ever loved, or ever will love, and I want you to marry me."

That is all right. But how much greater is the love that says, "I have met many people whom I have loved very much. I will undoubtedly love other people. *Knowing this,* I choose *you*—I ask *you* to share your life with me in marriage!"

I can think of no greater compliment. I also know of no finer credit that I could pay to my husband than to say, "Yes, aware of all the possibilities and potentials open to me, I commit my life to you in marriage."

The motive then for marriage rises above and beyond the emotional content of love alone and becomes a choice commitment.

I hope that you caught that key word: *commitment*. Commitment tears down the paltry excuses given today in the break-up of marriages. As the divorce rate escalates, it becomes evident that *commitment* got lost somewhere between the "I do" and "for better or for worse!"

More and more *Christian* marriages are brought to end on such bases as:

"I didn't plan for this to happen, but I met John and . . . I just can't help myself, I just love him so much."

"Mary has been a good wife, and I guess I still love her; but when Shirley came to work for me, we just hit it off great! We enjoy the same things, . . ." ad nauseam.

So? So you love. So you enjoy.

What about commitment?

I honestly believe that, when we reinstate the emphasis on *commitment* in marriage rather than just on *love,* we will provide a sounder basis upon which to build Christian homes.

The wider my experience with others, the more inconsistency I find in dealings with the marriage vows. Commitment keeps us wedded to political entities; commitment encourages us to take night classes, put in overtime, and brush up on "homework" to get ahead (or caught up!) in our jobs and professions. Then why are we so quick to throw in the towel when our marriages prove not to be so perfect or ideal?

Commitment is the cement that holds the marriage together.

At those times of weakness when (other) love may *constrain* us, commitment *restrains* us!

When love makes the world go 'round, commitment keeps us from getting dizzy!

Love may not have to say we're sorry—but commitment commands apology.

* * *

I mentioned earlier that Manget and I, in reassessing our own marriage, learned many lessons that have served to strengthen our union. In addition to accepting the fact that it is possible and even probable that we could genuinely love many people, we have learned that making a marriage is a full-time job. In other words, we work at it.

We do our homework; we try for some bonus points. We no longer coast along on the basis of vows made twenty-five years ago; rather, we recognize the need for a constant renewal of those vows. "I take you *this day* to be my. . . ." *Every day!*

Together we have also learned one of the whys of our experience. Prior to my own personal temptation, and even during that time, I was quite certain that I stood totally alone among Christian community.

However, shortly after we went through our own Gethsemane experience, I found that I had not been alone. In a most remarkable way, people began to come to us with similar problems. These Christian friends— and sometimes strangers—approached us with what became a familiar, "There is no one I can talk to about this, but somehow I feel like you will understand."

The truth of 2 Corinthians 1:3-4 became active in our lives. "Blessed be God, even the Father of our Lord Jesus Christ, the Father of mercies, and the God of all comfort; Who comforteth us in all our tribulation, *that we may be able to comfort them which are in any trouble,* by the comfort wherewith we ourselves are comforted of God" (author's italics.)

We had surely been allowed to go through a dark hour of temptation in order that we might genuinely understand and minister to others in like circumstances. Out of personal experience, we could say, "I *know* how you feel. I know the temptation. But I also know that the Bible is true, that 'there hath no temptation taken you but such as is common to man: but God . . . will not suffer you to be tempted above that ye are able; but will with the temptation also make a way to escape' " (1 Cor. 10:13).

There also came a new understanding and love toward those who succumb to temptation and do not come out unscathed.

One young couple whom we know suffered through the heartbreak of divorce. While tongues wagged and unmerciful judgment was passed upon them, we walked with them. We shared their frustrations, their struggles, and their tears. We prayed with them and for them. While well-meaning Christians turned their backs, we held their hands. While co-workers criticized, we agonized. Now they have both gone their separate ways. Perhaps one of the highest compliments paid us was in a letter from the young woman.

She wrote: "I know that at no time did you ever like or approve of my actions. But through all of the hurt and agony of this decision, I have known that you were not judging me. You were loving me and praying for me. I shall always be grateful. Thank you."

I believe that in the context of this unhappy ending of a marriage, where temptation took its toll, this is a good place to really look at the subject. Temptation is an often misunderstood subject in Christian experience.

In regard to temptation, as in my own experience, we speak too quickly. Experientially, quite often, we "know not whereof we speak!" Our judgmental attitudes are more often the result of ignorance than of conviction.

I am reminded of the young woman in my mission

group in Guyana. We were discussing the subject of temptation and in that case, dealing with sexual experience. Joline prided herself in that just the previous week she had "overcome temptation." The lovely Indian girl went on to relate the incident.

"The man in charge of the shop where I work called me into his office. He told me that if I would grant certain 'favors' for him that evening after work, I would get a promotion." Joline smiled, and added proudly, "I told him no and went out of the office." The girl then turned to the group and said, "So you see, we do not have to give in when we are tempted."

I appreciated her testimony but recognized the danger of her apparent confidence, so I asked her, "Joline, did you like the man at all?"

"No," she said, defiantly. "I can't stand him! Nobody at work likes him."

"Then you really had no desire to be with the man, regardless of the financial benefits?" I queried.

"Absolutely not!" she said with finality.

"Then you really were not faced with what the Bible refers to as real temptation," I offered.

I went on then, as now, to explain that in studying temptation in the Scripture, there are two elements which must be present: *desire* and *opportunity*. Without both we do not encounter real temptation. Joline had the opportunity, but not the desire. So she was not actually tempted.

A good case in point was the eighteen-year-old girl, suffering an advanced case of acne, who was also carrying around about seventy-five pounds of excess weight. The obvious social reject stood up in the youth meeting and avowed with outward conviction, "I believe that it is a moral sin for a Christian to dance. I would never do it!" Looking at her, one knew she had never been asked! She had never had the opportunity. (The mischief in me secretly wished that the captain of the football team would ask her to the homecoming dance—*then* let her give her testimony!)

The life of Jesus Christ brings home the truth of this concept of desire and opportunity as these issues relate to temptation. The temptations of Jesus as recorded in the Gospels demonstrate the awesome power of these two factors.

In each of the three faces of temptation, Satan appealed to Jesus on the basis of *desire* and sought to destroy him through the avenues of *opportunity*.

Jesus was hungry. He had been in the wilderness and had fasted for forty days. He desired food. Had he not been hungry, the opportunity of turning stones to bread would have had no appeal whatsoever. Jesus was tempted physically, emotionally, and spiritually—in areas of need following the time of aloneness and isolation in the wilderness. He had strong personal desires, and because he was God incarnate, he certainly had opportunity to fulfill those desires. But, being tempted, he overcame.

Again, we could walk with Jesus into the garden of Gethsemane. Perhaps His greatest hour of temptation lay here. By His very words, Jesus had a *desire* to live. By His divine being, He had the *opportunity* to live. But because of His commitment to do not His will, but the will of the Father, Jesus did not yield to temptation. I personally contend that the agonizing groans from Gesthemane far outweighed the cries from Calvary. The decision to accept the cup was far more difficult than the drinking of it.

Only when one has "been to the garden" and faced the trial of temptation and knows the sheer agony of submitting to God's will above personal desire and opportunity can one understand failure in the lives of others. You can be sure that those who have drunk from the cup of submission will be the *last* to bring judgment and condemnation upon a weaker brother or sister.

Paul Tournier in his book *Guilt and Grace* said that one could not boast of faithfulness until he had been tempted to unfaithfulness and remained faithful.

"Faithfulness without temptation to infidelity is not true faithfulness. Faith without temptation to doubt is not true faith. Purity without temptation to impurity is not true purity."[1]

Manget has often illustrated the point of desire and opportunity in relation to temptation in this way: A man proudly states that he has overcome temptation to drinking hard liquor. "I passed right by the store and didn't even stop," the man asserts, adding, "I just really never did like the stuff anyway."

His friend, a struggling alcoholic, passes the same store. It is payday, and his salary envelope is in his pocket. The man stops and gazes into the liquor store, bottles glinting in the afternoon sunlight, beckoning buyers. His hand in his pocket tightens its grip on the pay envelope. Familiar smells and feelings rise up in his throat. An inner prayer for strength pulsates in the man's throat. With finality, he turns and walks away, home to his family.

The first man was not tempted. He had opportunity but actually no desire for the liquor. His idea of having "overcome temptation" was false.

The second man was sorely tempted. He had a deep desire for the drink, and he had the opportunity to fulfill that desire. But by the power of God within him, he overcame the temptation!

We can spend our lifetime watching ships pass by on

the sea of life, and we can say proudly and with certainty, "I would never set my sail in that direction." But only when we get out of dry dock, onto the oceans of experience, and set our own sails into the wind, can we put the ships of our faith to the real test.

A dear friend of mine has a wall plaque in her office which I love. It reads, "Before you criticize, abuse, or accuse, walk a mile in my shoes."

Among the *nevers* of my life lies a lesson lately learned: In times of temptation, whether by God's grace we overcome, or before his face we fall, we have the assurance from his word that "Though he fall, he shall not be utterly cast down, for the Lord upholdeth him with his hand" (Ps. 37:24).

"Underneath are the everlasting arms" (Deut. 33:27).

And he will never leave us when we fall.

Never.

8

I Know We Are Supposed to Love Everybody . . .
I Could Never Love Anybody Like That!

The first time I saw her, I thought I would be sick. Her name was Shirlee.

If she is *a she,* I questioned, and then rebuked myself. But her appearance made one wonder.

We were working with the Golden Grove Baptist Church in Guyana. I had survived the culture shock resulting from planting myself—a child of the deep South—into a totally black Caribbean culture.

In fact, that particular morning I was inwardly congratulating myself because I had been able to leave the van, step over and around the dung droppings in the road, and had crossed the trench without turning up my nose in recognition of that ever-present odor which emanated from the "water system" in the village. Now, before you pin blue ribbons on me, the stench was still there—and inwardly I was all but gagging—but outwardly I wore a look of serene acceptance. This time *I* was first to extend my hand to greet the smiling Christians who gathered in the little converted (literally!) rum shop where we held our worship services.

I met all the cheery greetings with ease and had just settled on the rough plank bench inside the little wooden building to wait for the worship service to begin. And she came in.

It was one of those times when you practice the fine

84

West Indian art of "looking without looking." I saw her—and quickly looked away.

But I held the grotesque mass of humanity in one corner of my eye. Shirlee had the features and body of a woman—yet there were masculine markings. From her chin grew a dark curling beard; her remaining few teeth were huge and terribly decayed. They protruded in every direction, preventing her from closing her lips. Saliva ran from the corners of her misshapen mouth and oozed into the tangled beard.

The ugliness of her gnarled hands was surpassed only by her twisted, near-crippled feet. Bones grew where there should have been no bones; the feet were so horribly deformed that no shoes could possibly have ever been worn.

To add misery to miseries, a most rank and foul odor emanated from this freakish fault from some female womb.

I caught my breath; the stench of human feces was near me. I sensed her nearness as the twisted feet shuffled along, closer to my bench. Finally, I was forced to look up.

Bright, vacant eyes, reflecting mental deficiency, stared down at me. A broad smile covered half of her face, and saliva dripped from the distorted mouth. Wild, untamed hair twisted in several directions. I tried to look away.

Both my hands tightened on my purse and gripped my Bible. Oh, God, no! I was choking inwardly. Not this.

But it was happening. Nature's mistake was sliding beside me on the bench.

I tried to ignore the presence. I refused to look in her direction. Then coarse, sandpapery fingers brushed my arm.

I turned.

Knotty, twisted fingers reached out to shake my hand. Innocent insanity mumbled something that sounded like a vaguely coherent "Goo' mornin'."

I responded with a light touch of the hand. I slid further away, closer to the children who were with me. (I might add that Tim and Jeff were older, and they were both cow-eyed with intrigue over this person to whom they would always refer as "the Lady with the beard.")

The worship service began. I was actually trembling with distaste and anger. Distaste because of the obvious stink (sorry, there is no polite word that will do here) pervading *my* premises; anger because I felt God had truly made a mistake. I was certainly the neatest, cleanest, smartest, best-dressed woman in church. And now the raunchiest, dirtiest, dumbest, and most pitiful piece of person had *dared* to sit with me!

Tears actually smarted in my eyes. As I pulled myself into a knot to avoid physical contact, I knew one thing: *God* may love the whole world, but I was not God! I might be supposed to love everyone, but one thing was certain: I could NEVER love anyone like that!

Everyone was gathered around us, saying good-bye. Tears were flowing freely—both from Manget and me and from the eyes of our beautiful Guyanese friends. We were saying farewell to a chapter in our life that had grown deeply, and it hurt. The friends we had come to know and love wept openly and unabashedly in their own sadness over our departure.

As they hugged us and cried and pledged prayers, I was momentarily caught up in a sea of emotion. Then I realized that there was a bit of a commotion near me. I looked up.

There stood Shirlee. The poor, pitiable woman was dragging her stubbled feet, reaching out toward me, big tears rolling down her cheeks.

The other women of the church had seen Shirlee as she sought to follow their example. One friend, Velma, had attempted to come to my rescue and caught Shirlee's arm. She restrained her and turned the dirty, weeping, half-witted woman away.

"No!" I spoke loudly, "Please, Velma, no. Let her come." And in an unforgettable moment, Shirlee came to me, put her gnarled hands in mine, and kissed me on the cheek.

And I know that, by God's grace, I truly did love that one whom I thought that I could never love.

You see, God keeps teaching us about Himself, and His ways are so far above our ways, that sometimes we think: He just does not know *this* situation or He would never have expected me to love him or her or them. Or, in that particular case—Shirlee.

The tremendous beauty of that parting moment could not be understood by just anyone. I do not know if I could even convey the total implications in mere words. Following my initial encounter with the "village idiot" I had come, step by step, to know compassion, caring, and even love. As she would hand me a hymnal to find the number (after I would turn it right side up), she would open her mouth and moan a monotone cadence as we all sang. She would continually look up to me and grin that pathetic witless grin, seeking my own smile in return.

The fact that, in the final day, such a person could feel the freedom to come, just like everyone else, to bid me farewell, and then demonstrate such a profound display of emotion, was for me a triumphant moment: In spite of my own personal inadequacies, God's love had come through!

And that would not have ever happened, had it not been for a lesson in love learned a few years earlier. The occasion was a "proof text" of God's love, demonstrated in real life.

The day had been typical, as were the events that occurred. It was early fall, and the leaves had been falling daily in golden confusion over the yard. Manget had promised to get his afternoon visitation done and start raking (so that the pastorium could pass inspection of the critical nonchurched neighbors, who paid great attention to such matters).

I had taught school all week and celebrated the TGIF syndrome (Thank Goodness It's Friday) enjoyed by teachers and students alike. I had brought the boys home from school, gotten Jon from the sitter, and unloaded all the Friday afternoon accumulation. Finally, everyone home and in place, happy husband rescuing us from neighborhood disgrace by removing nature's colorful carnage from the towering oaks, I kicked off my shoes and settled on the sofa for my much-deserved time of do-absolutely-nothing-and-make-no-apology-I-don't-care!

No sooner had I "unlaxed" when Manget called out to me from the side door. "Hey, Honey—don't look now, but here comes Irene."

Irene. *Oh, no! Not that addle-brained, gossipy, old busybody,* I thought. *Not her. Not today. She knows I just got home.*

My thoughts and conclusions continued in head-on collisions as I looked out the window and saw her coming up the walk. Her head held high, her chin jutted out in that usual haughty, but pious manner, Irene was taking a broad, determined stride up the front walk.

A leader in our Sunday School, a strong singer in the choir, an active women's missionary worker—in everyone of these positions she held a lofty self-appointed position: chief critic. Therefore, I had come to just one conclusion—I hated her guts.

That is crude, but . . . that's it. Never, not once, had I ever heard Irene say anything good about anyone or anything. No matter who or what came up, all the joy and enthusiasm with which one began would soon be dampened. Irene just seemed to thrive on pessimism and disillusionment. If a new person came into the church, Irene was the first to the pastor—and subsequently to everyone else—to bring all the "background information" which she was convinced was her godly duty to share.

Now this ever-unwelcome guest was once again at my door. Even my best friend would have been less than welcomed at that moment, but—alas my visitor was someone I despised.

With my shoes back on, a push at my hair, I went to the door and opened it.

Wearing my warmest smile, my most radiant "glow," and a mental rerun of my lines, I greeted her. "Irene! How *lovely* to see you! Do come in. . . ." And in further response to her courtesy questions, "Oh, no, not at all! I just came in and have plenty of time. . . ."

While inwardly I was approaching chemical combustion, outwardly I was a shining example of saccharin sweetness, dispensing God's love and portraying the Perfect Pastor's Wife. *No one* could have known otherwise.

Except me.
And God.

Later that evening it continued to bother me. I talked to Manget about it. He understood my personal dislike of Irene, but I told him that it went deeper than that.

"I don't love her," I retorted, "and I am *supposed* to," I wailed. "When God gave the Commandment, *she* had never been born," I contended, half-humorous, half-serious.

Later that night I lay awake in bed still struggling with my own feelings. In the days that followed, the more encounters I had with Irene, the greater grew my hostility and negative feelings. At the same time, the more I grew to dislike her, the more I "faked" that real Christian love which I was *supposed* to have.

As I neared a crisis period—a breaking point—I knew I could go on no longer with people talking about what a "warm and loving person" I was, while I harbored actual hate in my heart for a Christian. Finally, in desperation, I went before God and acknowledged my fault.

No, first of all, I acknowledged *her* faults! "Oh, God, I am sure you understand how bossy . . . how haughty . . . how pious . . . that wagging, gossiping tongue. . . ." But wait. No, I had to start over.

"God," I tried again, "you know that I do not exactly care for Irene like I should. . . ."

That would not do either. I backed up. I felt so ashamed, but I went on: "God, I can't stand that woman! I hate her! I hate what she does to others; I hate what she does to me. . . ." And suddenly I really did see what was happening to *me*. "I know that I am supposed to love everyone—but I *cannot* bear that woman!" And I honestly told God that I did not want to have those feelings.

I sat quietly for awhile, and then it seemed that God

began to speak to me through my thoughts. In the next few minutes, He gave me the most marvelous release from the *agape* act which I had been performing for His benefit. He set me free.

It was as though His voice were echoing through the very corridors of my soul. "I know. I know that you do not love Irene. But, you see, Elaine, *I* love her. I loved her enough to die for her. And I live in *you*. Now, you just *stop trying*. Quit faking it. Relax, and just continue to let me *live* in you—and I will *love* in you!"

Nothing in the realm of my total Christian experience has ever been more liberating! I was free! *I* did not *have* to love Irene. I just had to love Jesus Christ and *let Him love*. I did not know how or when but I suddenly knew that I was sincerely going to love Irene.

It did not happen overnight. But step by step, day by day, it happened. The beginning was me. I stopped faking it. Game time was over. The next time I saw Irene, I was me. Polite, cordial, real. Me.

It was almost unbelievable. When I threw away my script and no longer had to spend my time concentrating on the lines my "role" had demanded, I began to *listen*. And as I really did listen, with both my ears and my heart, I began to know Irene. Emotions emerged and realities revealed, and Irene became a *person*.

In a matter of weeks, I found myself deeply caring, genuinely concerned, and even surprised myself by going to her house one afternoon. A short time later Irene's husband became very ill, and I led the entourage of casseroles and cleaning to keep the family going during the crisis. As she sat in her kitchen and wept over the severity of the problem, suddenly I was washed with a shocking revelation: I loved her!

It is of significance that even to this day I confess and acknowledge that I never did particularly *like* the woman. I would not choose to spend time with her for enjoyment, family fun, or conversational pleasure. It would never happen. We are miles apart in personality, background, and basic interests. But I do love her. God in me has brought this to pass. I feel a love that weeps with her when she weeps, rejoices with her when she rejoices. It is a love that shares what I have with her in her need, a love that prays for God's very best in her life, and that leaps to her defense before her critics.

It was such a beginning in the Lord's lessons of love in my own heart that has carried me beyond the stage of a false façade to embrace the rather earthen realities of life and love.

Some persons we just love automatically; others we must turn to God and very frankly confess our lack. When we talk straight to God, He has a refreshing way of talking straight back to us! He enables us—by His very presence being Love itself—to love the unlovely.

And *the lovely*.

Very few people really think about this. Loving Shirlee and accepting her as a person—still caring to this day, often wondering about her—was not easy. Learning to love Irene, basically an unlovely person by her manner and character, was difficult. Studies and programs and lessons and pulpit challenges to love the unlovely are not uncommon.

Is it possible that we channel our outreach efforts toward "loving the unlovely" at the exclusion of loving the *lovely?*

There are thousands of broken, lonely, lovely people in our world. Their lives appear full, but their hearts are empty; their days exclude excitement, but their nights are excruciating; their smiles are plastic, but their tears are very real. And, like the unlovely people of this world, lovely people are lost.

I do not know exactly what it is, but for some reason the "dedicated Christian society" rushes with open arms to reach out to and undergird the unlovely in our communities. This is 100 percent right. But it is also 100 percent right to lift the lovely to our God!

Could it be that we enjoy a false sense of pride, or does personal insecurity cause us to shy away from those often referred to as "the beautiful people"? Are we unknowingly threatened by them? Is it easier to struggle with teeming masses unloading from church buses or to walk beside a stumbling, struggling alcoholic, knowing that these people will most likely never be reaching up to overshadow us in the church or community? Can we have so much personal pride in our position that we hesitate to give our energies to one who might just possibly rise above us in leadership or in faith?

Ouch!

God has ways of dealing with us and our pride—and often we are left crushed and broken. And, paradoxically, whole.

One of the most ego-shattering experiences of my own life happened in relation to this very thing: loving the unlovely—and the lovely!

We long planned for and I coordinated a Christian Arts Festival on our beautiful island of Grenada. Christian professionals in the performing, visual, and technical arts came to the island and presented the gospel through the arts. It was a magnificent week: culturally enriching, spiritually dynamic, and an event which unified people from all walks of life. The Christian Arts Festival is still talked about today.

Among the guests for the week was Jeannette Clift. The talented actress who had portrayed Corrie ten Boom in the movie, *The Hiding Place*, had not only appeared on stage and given her testimony at our premiere of that film, but she had presented dramatic monologues at the culture center during the festival. Her husband, Lorraine George, had accompanied her. For both of them, it had been a spiritually uplifting time. Before they left, Jeannette gave me a gift. A tiny pendant of "The Hiding Place—in God's Hands" which she had designed and silversmith James Avery had cast. There had been twelve of this particular item made, and the cast destroyed. As she left the precious ornament with me, she told me the story and noted that, at my receiving it, I was getting the fifth of the twelve. She owned one. The other three persons who, at that time, had received such a gift from her, were all internationally known Christians of much honor and significance. I was overwhelmed!

The more I thought about it, the more pride came into my life. I wore my silver pendant for a few weeks—until everyone had seen it. And, of course, until I had been able to tell my nice story to everyone! I managed to wear it most conspicuously or "finger it" until someone would ask! After I had gotten all the mileage out of it that I needed, I put it away in my jewelry box. (Not without a most prideful thank you to God for this great honor, pleased that He knew how much I deserved it!)

Months passed. In March 1979, Manget left the island for a preaching mission to Guyana. On the night of March 12, Jon and I went routinely to bed. In a predawn coup on the morning of March 13, our little island nation was plunged into revolution. In a matter of hours a friend lay shot in the street; the country was in an uproar. Phone lines for all overseas calls were shut down; wire services stopped; the airport closed. Manget could not get home! Although we were in no real immediate danger, we were completely shut off from the rest of the world.

Planes did not fly in for five days. We stayed home. God had miraculously sent some houseguests (*they* didn't fully appreciate my "miracle"!). Since they could not leave, we were not alone. But it was awesome and frightening to see our harbored haven suddenly alive with armed militia of the pro-Cuban regime which had toppled the postcolonial dictatorship and was openly embracing Communism.

For two days and nights I did not sleep. I would lie in bed at night and listen to the staccato of gunfire in the distance. I would stand by my window and watch trucks load and unload armed guards who were to patrol the beach below our house. At midnight, they would fire off a round of shots before they changed the guard.

In this atmosphere, charged with fear and apprehension, anxiety and depression began to erode my personal faith. Mentally I was shaking my fist in God's face, saying, "I did not want to be a missionary in the first place! I did what I thought You wanted—I came! And now look what You let us get into!" Now, that was not very nice, and I am sure that all of "those who sent us out" would have handled it much better. But I blew it. I was quite angry with God.

In such a mood of pessimism and defeat, I walked into my room and stood by the dresser. Suddenly my eyes fell on the jewelry case. I opened it. Lying against the brown velvet lining was the silver pendant. "The Hiding Place in God's Hands."

I was momentarily stricken. I picked up the tiny piece of silver. Oh, how could I? How could I! Just months before I had flaunted this objet d'art upon my person with great pride. That moment tears began to come. *Oh, God,* I cried out silently, *forgive me.*

I had not received that pendant because I was *somebody.* God had placed that in my hands because He saw, in His omniscience, this hour of my need. He knew that I, too, would need a reminder that He alone was my "hiding place."

I wore the pendant again—on a longer chain, hidden from view, lest I succumb to pride. It is a personal reminder that God is my hiding place—but an even greater reminder that it is easy to let personal pride keep us from knowing God's best!

And it is still a reminder to me of one of God's greatest I AMs, love. Reminding me that the love which invades our lives—*agape* love—is not always a feeling. It is a fact. It is a decision that I make: I let God love through me. Those whom I can *never* love—He can! He already does!

When lack of love tries to rule our hearts with defeat, we embrace a *never* from the writing of the psalmist: In love . . . "Never let me be defeated" (Ps. 31:1, GNB).

If Illness Like That
Ever Came to Our Family . . .
I Could Never Handle It!

From my impressionable preteen years and on into somewhat mature adulthood, I have had a fear of and an aversion to serious illness. Perhaps because it was my good fortune to grow up in an exceptionally healthy family or maybe for some other reason, but illness was a stranger to me. None of my immediate family was ever in the hospital, and the only sickness that we knew in our home was an occasional bout with the flu or a bad cold.

Once in a while, I would come into contact with friends outside the family who faced serious illness and often long-term struggles with life-and-death situations. I always shied away from such people, preferring to "put them on my prayer list" in lieu of my visitation or telephone list!

As a pastor's wife, I can recall vividly a few specific situations where I gallantly offered to "sit here in the car and pray" while my minister husband made personal visits to the seriously ill church members. It wasn't that I did not care. I did. I cared very, very much. My personal caring was perhaps deeper than that of the average person. But, regretably, I did not know what to say or what to do. I have never been in the midst of or close enough to serious illness to understand or know what to do. Or what to say. Or, of prime importance, what to *think*.

A very dear friend of mine phoned the house one Thanksgiving Day. Sara and her husband, Billy, had carried their three-year-old son to the doctor. Young Philip had suffered for several days with a bad cold, and he was not recovering at all. In a matter of a few hours, Sara's world turned over.

Philip had leukemia.

Manget went to the hospital immediately and later spent many hours with our friends. Claiming no answers about why the young Christian couple should suddenly face such a crisis, Manget asked Bill and Sara to join him in a commitment: Trusting everything to God, they would take life *one day at a time*.

On several occasions, Philip hung between life and death. As months went by, trips to Saint Jude's Hospital in Memphis brought both hope and despair to Sara and Bill. Hope—because the latest drugs and treatment offered their son a fighting chance; despair—because week after week the young couple saw other children die with the same disease which gripped their own child.

One day Sara called me and with much enthusiasm shared her latest finding. "I may not know all the reasons for this, but I do know one," she offered. "I am going through this experience so that I can understand and help others go through it!" Sara went further to tell me that, while in Memphis the previous week for Philip's chemotherapy, she was reading the Bible and came upon the Scripture in 2 Corinthians 1:3-4. "I can say truthfully to others, 'I *do* know what you are going through . . . I am there!' " My friend went on to say that every week she had a chance to share her hope and her faith with some other broken, hurting, anxious parent at Saint Jude's.

I hung up the telephone after offering, weakly, "That's wonderful, Sara. I am so glad." Wonderful? Her son, the same age as my healthy, bubbly, laughing Jon, is possibly *dying*, and she can talk like that?

My heart felt strangely comforted by her words; yet I sensed now, more than ever, my own inadequacy. Sara was "just a housewife": she had worked from time to time in public work, she kept the church nursery with me on "every third Sunday," and she sang in the choir. Why, she wasn't even a Sunday School teacher! And here she was in the midst of one of life's cruelest battles—and she was on top!

By contrast, there I stood: a minister's wife; a Sunday School teacher; a counselor for youth; an educated, somewhat talented person, equipped for life. Or so I had thought.

Until now.

I walked away from the phone, Sara's joy convicting my heart. "Come to see me," she had added. Again. And my numb and meaningless reply: "Yes, of course." *Again.* My friend was fighting bravely in the battlefield of crisis and tragic illness. And I was AWOL!

I just could not go. I could not bear to see that wasted child, now pale and bald from cancer treatments, purple veins and gums, weakened and helpless. The reality of sickness and suffering was too evident in that house.

Manget could visit. He was more understanding toward me than perhaps he should have been. But he went. And I would pray. Oh, and I did pray! I prayed for that family until the tears would stay no more. And I continued to pray. But I could not go.

That was fourteen years ago. Today Philip is seventeen years old and is as big and as strong and as robust as our own son Jon. Philip is a miracle of God's power and of his parents' endeavors and of many prayers—and of God's hand at work through modern medical science.

Yet I recall vividly telling Manget about Sara's phone call that memorable afternoon. "She's hurting, but she is fantastic about it! I just don't know how she does it. If anything like that ever came to our family, well, I could never handle it!

After more years of missionary service, we came home again from overseas.

We had looked forward to our leave time again in the U.S. We would have a few months with our son, Jeff, during the summer before his senior year in college. We would get to *meet* our new daughter-in-law! Tim and Vicky had met and married while we were abroad, and military duties had prevented our having occasion to meet them before our return home. And Manget and I would both be home to see Jon graduate from high school.

Home from the islands. We were jubilant!

America! Reunion with family and friends. Opportunity for work and ministry in Atlanta. So many reasons for gratitude, and a multitude of plans stretched out before us for the weeks and months ahead.

However, near the top the list of "first things" lay that necessary interruption—a medical examination which our mission board requires of all personnel returning home after service overseas.

Admittedly, we had a few not-too-missionary-sounding words for that part of our schedule. With so many things to do, it was certainly understandable that we found such a requirement to be unreasonable and certainly unnecessary for us. Why should we take time out of our daily life and subject ourselves to a few days of being punched, poked, plundered, photographed? Especially when we had no problems.

An extensive physical exam was a waste of time and money for people like us who looked and felt great. Manget related a statement from a current magazine which expounded upon the extravagance of what was becoming termed as "unnecessary routine examinations" for healthy people with no complaints. In fact, when we first scheduled appointments with the doctors, my busy husband (who much preferred traveling and speaking to congregations over against posturing and posing for the physicians) told me quite firmly: "I am *not* going for this physical. It just really is not necessary. You go ahead and go—you do need to see the gynecologist about those female complaints that you have had from time to time. I will wait and go later on."

He was determined.

But so was I.

With my lifelong aversion to anything or any place that even faintly smelled of "medical," I certainly had no intentions of going through some three days of exhaustive, intensive physical examination alone.

I am still not certain just what changed his mind. Either I was quite persuasive, or maybe it was the memories of previous physicals—being draped in rough, white surgical gowns, grasping them together behind us as we stumbled, blue-purple-chilled along the sterile passageways of X-ray—an unforgettable sensual delight I am sure! But whatever it was, when the time came, Manget agreed to go on and have his physical along with me.

The Thursday afternoon that my gynecologist phoned to tell me that my biopsy had been negative and that I was the recipient of "a lovely report," I was delighted. I can remember walking around the house singing the doxology all afternoon.

Late that same afternoon a phone call came with Manget's report. There seemed to be some sort of problem. He was seriously anemic and more tests would be run. A dark cloud settled over our household.

Four days and a battery of tests later, Manget came into the house, laid an envelope of X-rays on the piano, and collapsed on the side of the bed in tears. The X-rays and blood tests and CAT scan had produced an educated opinion: "Very likely we are dealing with cancer."

That first afternoon we cried together briefly. Then in a most amazing way, we began immediately to draw from the numerous resources which were within our grasp.

In relating subsequent events, I once told someone that "we were totally unprepared" for what happened. I quickly retracted that statement. "No, no. Not 'unprepared.' It was totally *unexpected*, but we *were* prepared!" Miraculously, God had prepared us.

I had said that I could *never* cope if such a thing invaded our lives and our home. Contrariwise, beginning in September 1982, God once again conquered the unbearable weakness of my never.

In the days that followed we went through a biopsy, cancer surgery, received reports of metastases to the liver and lower stomach lining, and entered into a prolonged program of chemotherapy.

And we are making it!

Just as the covenant which Manget had entered into with Sara and Billy, we, too, are living life one day at a time. And we are loving the living of it!

Ways that our never-failing God has proven to be all that we ever hoped or believed him to be are too numerous to recount. We do know that he is truly "able to do exceeding abundantly above all that we ask or think" (Eph. 3:20).

Manget is just one of the one in every four Americans who has or will eventually have cancer. Yet do not be confused. He is not a statistic. He is a person. He is not just a person; he is my very special person. He is the man to whom I committed my life in marriage twenty-seven years ago. He is the person who has laughed with me and loved me, cried with me and loved me, been totally disgusted with me and loved me, encouraged me and loved me, been angry with me and loved me. In other words, he has been an integral part of my life.

Together we charted many an unknown course and came through victoriously. Life gave us lemons, and we made a lot of lemonade! And, conversely, life gave us lemonade and in our stumbling ignorance we produced some real lemons! God allowed us no special exemptions from the fears, frustrations, and dilemmas that most of the world faces; but He did give us His grace and His power in the midst of everything.

Just as He taught us so much through marriage, through our children, and through our professional lives, God is using our present crisis to teach us and reveal even more of Himself.

In those aforementioned ways that are above our understanding, God prepared us to look at cancer *head-on* and not panic.

It is true. First, you do cry. You cry because it hurts. The sheer emotional pain that comes with the discovery of anything that is a life-or-death situation produces tears.

There were those initial, momentary tears of anger. Manget said, "Why me, Lord?" And I was saying, "Why him, and why NOT me?" Those are human reactions from very human people.

But we did not homestead in a valley of tears. The truth of Psalm 30:5 was a practical reality from the first day. Our weeping might last for a short night, but there was the promise of "joy . . . in the morning."

I sat in the hospital room following surgery and looked out over the city of Atlanta. I watched the beautiful Georgia capital—our own "Big A"—come alive by night as the shades of darkness gradually revealed the brilliance of the southern metropolis, suddenly a blazing electric skyline under a warm September sky.

I looked out over my little world that night and thought of the evil and wickedness that abounded. Contrary to what one might have thought, I did not sit and question, *Why? Why didn't this happen to some evil, wicked person? Why not the drunken man whose love for alcohol and a speeding car had killed a twenty-nine-year-old young woman? Why is not the child molester locked away in the city jail stricken with cancer? Why should it not be one of them instead of my husband lying here with one third of the colon gone, and cancer cells already invaded the liver and . . .?"*

No, I was not asking those questions. Rather, I sat and looked out at my world beyond the hospital room and literally praised God with all my heart.

—I praised him because He had brought us home for just such a time as this.

—I praised Him because in His omniscience He had prepared us for this hour.

—I praised him because, in the presence of this enemy, He had prepared a table before us!

Before we left the island of Grenada we had seen, almost incidentally, a promotional flyer for a book entitled *Imaging* by Norman Vincent Peale. I ordered that book, not having a single clue as to what it contained, and had it sent to our stateside address.

That book which deals extensively with the process of guided spiritual imagery in the realm of physical healing, as well as in other areas of life, was awaiting us when we arrived in the States. Manget and I had both read the book during our first weeks back.

Out of curiosity, Manget had purchased another book at the local bookstore, The title? *When Bad Things Happen to Good People* by Harold S. Kushner.

Through the first book, *Imaging,* we had been reminded anew of the proven power of positive thoughts and the latent power which lies within each of us as we participate in our own health. Rabbi Kushner's book had reinforced that which we already knew—bad things happen to good people just as surely as good things happen to bad people!

These books upon our shelves, their messages fresh upon our minds, were a part of God's preparation for us. From the very afternoon that the word *cancer* invaded our lives, the tears were almost immediately replaced by two things: affirmation and understanding. There was the affirmation that God had not changed, that His power was still available; there was the understanding that no one is exempt from evil and wickedness in this world but that God would not forsake us in our hour of desperate need.

The following weeks are a blurred panorama of what, when, and how. I do know that the following day, after that strong inference of cancer was made by the doctor, Manget went to the magazine rack and began thumbing through the periodicals. "There was an issue of a newsmagazine I saw last week . . . here it is!" he exclaimed enthusiastically. It was another one of those things that he "just happened to have read." The article that he showed me was "Why More Americans are Surviving Cancer" in *U.S. News and World Report.*

Avidly we read and reread the informative and encouraging report. I placed it out for ready reference. As our pilgrimage began, we held tenaciously to the hope that was offered by today's medicine. We clung to an understanding that illness and pain are a part of this world that we live in, and there is the promise that such does not come from God. To the effects of sin and evil in this world, no person is exempt.

Not even us.

Nor you.

Thus as the days and weeks went by, we found ourselves among the tens of thousands of other people in today's world who are facing and living with a dreaded disease. Where I had so selfishly thought that I simply could not do it, like so many other situations where "I can't," *He can.* I am fully aware that the sum total of my ability to cope and my dear husband's ability not only to cope but to face and to faith and to fight comes from that divine power within—and around us.

During the past months we have learned so many things. Some of those things are new truths, others are past-known facts which have been resurrected for this particular time. Some we knew theoretically but not experientially—until now.

We know the healing power of the Word of God. The psalmist said, "He sent his word, and healed them" (Ps. 107:20). There is something inexplicably potent about the Word of God. As much as we love to read, the Bible has top priority in our lives. I have already shared the blessing and stabilizing influence of other books. In no way would I discredit or eliminate the value and power of good reading. I not only acknowledge it—I applaud

it! In fact, following surgery, Manget found the book
Getting Well Again by Dr. Carl Simonton to be second
only to the Bible in getting him oriented into a recovery attitude. Every cancer patient and his/her family
should read it!

However, we must recognize that God's Word has a
unique place in the life of every Christian. In hours of
crisis, fear, sadness, and when I am tempted to discour-
agement, the Word of God has sustained me.

After the medics had performed the biopsy on Manget, we had to wait and wait. Up until that time, even
though everything had pointed and indicated malignancy, there was still a tiny edge for error, a hope
against hope, a margin for reprieve, that professional
speculation and today's technology could be wrong. "It
could be a parasite from your tropical island that is
giving us this reading," the doctor had once suggested,
"I doubt it very seriously, but . . . we'll just have to get
that biopsy report."

As any sane person would have done, I clutched that
incidental statement like a drowning person must
reach for a rope, clinging to that slim thread of hope,
rejecting the strong probability of dreaded disease.
From day one, we had thought positively. *Don't write
it down yet . . . let's pray for the best.* But all the while,
lurking in the back of my mind, *What if it is? What will
I do? What will Manget do?* How quickly I forget! I
would not get the ticket until it was time to get on the
train!

In the midst of waiting hours, God's Word shone in
the darkness of my mind with consoling clarity. "[I] will
not be afraid of evil tidings [bad news]" (Ps. 112:7). I
read that verse again. I jumped up and literally shouted
it. I did not have to fear bad news. "Honey," I said to
my husband at his hospital bedside, "I read this two

ways. First, we have no need to sit around and worry and anticipate bad news. Second, if, in fact, it does come, we do not have to be afraid of it!"

In either case, we did not *have* to know fear.

And we did not.

Some people would find it hard to believe, but this is how that Scripture translated into life.

Friday morning before I could prepare Jon's breakfast and get back to the hospital, Manget phoned me from his room. He was his usual bright, cheerful self, greeting me with his husky, affected, sexy-sounding, "Good morning, Lover." Quickly following his "What's for breakfast?' " was a very matter-of-factly, offhanded statement: "The doctor was by this morning quite early. It is definitely malignant."

My mouth fell open, my heart did a flip-flop, and before I could say, "Oh, Honey . . ." he was on with it. "He says they'll do surgery and begin chemotherapy, and hopefully they'll be able to add a number of useful years to my life."

I swallowed. Finally it was my turn. "Oh, Honey . . . but . . . how *are* you?"

The peace and contentment was almost audible as it flowed in his voice. "Me? Oh, I'm fine. I just want to go on and get on with it!"

By the time I reached the hospital, Manget had already created quite a stir. He had danced circles with an austere head nurse, who had said, "You are crazy!" To which my husband had laughingly replied, "I may be, but it sure is fun!"

"I will not fear bad news."

We had our tickets.

We were on the train.

Another thing that has strengthened and renewed us

during this time is that *we have embraced the healing power of laughter.*

Certainly there have been tears. There has been pain. Physical pain, emotional pain, mental pain. Truthfully we would not hesitate to exchange illness for good health. That just is not our option right now. However, in the midst of our valley, we have not stopped laughing.

Actually, we had not thought anything about that until a friend came to visit us and pointed out to us that we were laughing. Laughter has always been a part of our lives, and we were somewhat startled when she said, "I cannot believe that you are able to laugh in the midst of this!"

Remember, I married a comedian. And he did too. Suddenly all of Manget's funny jokes, which I had often found inane and somewhat ridiculous, became rare gems in our day-to-day living. Then, perhaps it is because of our present situation, but I began to notice how many people are *not* laughing.

We noted this especially at Christmastime. While we were thanking God for and enjoying even two or three good hours when Manget felt strong enough to accompany me to the mall and walk about, doing a little shopping, we saw it. Time and again we encountered people, arms laden with parcels and brightly colored packages, scowling, and at times arguing with their companions.

While my never-to-be-stopped husband was buying his traditional "gag" gifts for family (which would be placed in marvelous boxes, concealing their identity and arousing the ultimate curiosity of all), we listened to the "happy holiday shoppers."

—"Well, she won't like it, no matter what. So I'll just get this, and she can bring it back."

—"One of these days I am going to draw the line. I'm sick and tired of trying to find him what he wants!"

—"I'm so tired of this mess . . . I'll be glad when Christmas is over!"

Frowning and raging and quarreling seemed to be the rule rather than the exception.

Where has all the laughter gone? How thankful I am for laughter and, more important, that we know the value of a laughing heart in the healing of both body and spirit.

It is interesting that a recent news story cited an art catalog accompanying the paintings of artist Jusepe de Ribera, a Spanish painter who lived 1588-1652. According to the catalog, "a contemporary ecclesiastic thought that laughing was 'the most Christian of facial expressions because it shows indifference to the trials of earthly existence.' "

I am prone to agree with the ancient ecclesiastic. *Laughter*. Real laughter. Not the plastic saccharin-sweet smiles, forced and affected by Christian personalities of "the media"—those smiles that belie the anger, doubt, fear, and sometimes lust that shines so clearly through the eyes. But laughter. Clear, sharp, clean laughter that expands the lungs, encourages the adrenaline, and "doctors" the mind, body, and spirit.

We were amazed, after our own discovery and "presumptions" about the healing effects that laughter had in our lives, to come across a book by Norman Cousins in which he deals at length with this same discovery!

We began the part of the program calling for the full exercise of the affirmative emotions as a factor in enhancing body chemistry. It was easy enough to hope and love and have faith, but what about laughter? . . . It worked. I made the joyous discovery that ten minutes of genuine belly laughter had an anesthetic effect and would give me at least two hours of pain-free sleep. . . .

How scientific was it to believe that laughter—as well as positive emotions in general—was effecting my body chemistry for the better? So we took sedimentation rate readings just before as well as several hours after the laughter episodes. Each time there was a drop of at least five points. The drop by itself was not substantial, but it held and was cumulative. I was greatly elated by the discovery that there is a physiologic basis for the ancient theory that laughter is good medicine.[2]

The "ancient theory" to which Mr. Cousins referred, is found recorded in Proverbs 17:22. The wise writer told us that "A merry heart doeth good like a medicine."

I may cry tonight. But I can burst into laughter moments later, and my broken heart and shattered spirit have mended once more.

A third factor and not of least importance to us has been the discovery of *the healing power of love.* God's love, our love for each other, and the expressed love of friends all combine to bring a sense of spiritual and physical healing.

From the day we first heard that we "most likely have cancer to deal with," and a minister friend from the church came over to spend a few minutes with us, up until this very hour, the love that others have shown has strengthened us in crisis.

As we have cherished every visit, every phone call, and every card expressing love and concern, I have realized how very foolish I was in years past to avoid those in the crisis of serious illness because "I just didn't know what to say." Memories at this moment which still strengthen me include many persons who *said nothing:* a dear friend who came to the hospital room and stood quietly, eyes brimming with tears, who walked over and squeezed my hand. Though her lips spoke no word, her spirit communicated with me in a way that few could understand. The fact that she came spoke louder than many words. She "didn't know what to say," but her presence told me that she cared tremendously.

Sometimes now days come that are just not good. Oh, yes! We do have them. Chemotherapy, while combating those cancer cells, takes its toll in sapping strength, producing nausea, and countless other ways can give the patient some pretty bad days! When those low days come, Manget takes a basket of cards which have come during the weeks and months since his surgery. As he sits and rereads the words and thoughts and encouragement offerred by loving friends, his spirit soars.

Occasionally he will call me to the living room, sitting there with those symbols of love and friendship, and will say, "With so much love and prayer, how can I lose?"

I consider this. And I answer from the depths of my soul. *You can't.*

We have God's love. "With his stripes *we are healed*" (Isa. 53:5, author's italics). We have that ever-growing love for each other. "In sickness and in health. . . ." And now those constant reminders that we are not bearing our burdens alone. Our friends are sharing the load.

When the doctors told Manget that he would be receiving chemotherapy treatments every week for a full year, he took the news with a very positive attitude. "Well, they expect me to be around for a year, anyway!" he laughed. And from the first day of treatment, he fixed in his mind that the "chemo" was going to be as bad for him as he let it. And it has been amazingly good to him.

Week after week he continues to go for treatments. There are the good days when he looks good and feels *almost* good. There are days when he is very weak and looks a bit haggard. As he puts it, "It's the pits!" From time to time, waves of nausea come and go. But he eats because he knows the value of good nutrition. He is tired, almost exhausted; but every day that the weather is clear, he takes a long walk. He sings and whistles and jokes with friends along the way.

And I am quite certain that sometimes he cries.

Because I cry.

I cry because I am unable to bear more of the burden for him.

I cry because he hurts and because he wants so desperately to feel really good again. And he can't. Not right now.

But he is making it. I believe that is because every day we awaken and one of us says aloud, "This is the day which the Lord hath made; we will rejoice and be glad in it." (Ps. 118:24).

In recent months God has allowed us to meet and visit firsthand with many others who have walked through the same valley where we are today—and they have emerged triumphantly to tell us about it. Others have not come through, and we are fully aware of that. But even many of those, with a proper concept of God, a positive attitude, and support from loving friends, lived their days with a *quality* of life that was far superior to many whose years were greater in number.

I cannot consider our family situation today without

drawing renewed strength from a memory. I remember Sara. And I remember Philip. When man had no hope, God had the last word. And today Philip still lives.

Monumental strides are being made in medical science every day. God uses people, our minds, medicine, and His own divine intervention in the course of nature to bring about healing.

Some burdens are only a bother; some are heavy; then, occasionally, the burden that befalls us is seemingly unbearable. We think that we can *never* handle it.

Then God reenters that particular scenario of life with another promise: He will *never* allow anything to come upon us except He give us the grace to bear it.

And, *always*, His grace is sufficient.

Afterword . . .
Never Alone

I saw the manuscript spilling from the brown envelope onto the floor beside the typewriter in the corner. It was difficult to look at.

My eyes were red and likely quite swollen from one of those unexpected bursts of tears. The manuscript suddenly screamed at me, as had so many other things recently.

"I'll have to rewrite that last chapter," I said aloud. "Everything has changed; it didn't work out, and now I will have to do it all over."

In a sudden, downhill turn of events, cancer had claimed my husband.

On May 7, 1983, Manget died.

I was alone.

I picked up the manuscript and sat back, staring ahead. I needed to read that last chapter, but it would hurt so very dreadfully. Yet there was something within drawing me to open the pages and read them one more time.

Inwardly I struggled with my own emotions but finally succumbed to the demands within my own mind. I reread chapter 9.

Then I knew that I would not change it. Not one word. It was that spirit of faith, hope, optimism, and commitment that had enabled us to laugh and to love our way through some otherwise heartbreaking days and weeks and months.

And it had been that same spirit that had enabled us to face life—and death—when the ominous verdict had been pronounced. Circumstances had not altered my commitment.

After severe attacks of intense pain, Manget was hospitalized. Further tests revealed that "the pain in the liver area" was caused by gallstones. We rejoiced. Surely that was good news.

"No," the surgeon informed us, "not good news. Quite possibly very bad news." He went on to explain to Manget, and later to the boys and me, that without the surgery the unbearable pain would continue, and there was the probability that the large number of stones would move and enter the pancreas. The surgery would be Manget's choice, and there was also the *possibility* that it could go all right.

Yet, the surgeon explained further, the possibility of complications "that could prove fatal" was great. Having to perform surgery right in the area of the liver, where the major metastasis was being treated, could cause a number of things to go wrong. He pointed out that any one or combination of adverse reactions could result in death.

So Manget had to make the decision.

He did not hesitate. "I cannot live with the pain. My life is in God's hands. There is no question. I will have the surgery."

Although the surgeon was greatly disappointed to discover that the liver metastasis was far more advanced than the X-rays had revealed, he felt that would in no way interfere with Manget's basic recovery from the surgery.

We went home from the hospital, still clinging to God's Word, surrounded by His love, bouyed by an unfailing faith, confidently praising Him for the healing we knew would come.

It did not come.

In less than a week, we knew we were in trouble. Fluid began to accumulate; Manget became increasingly disoriented. A one-week checkup revealed not only excessive fluids but also a severe jaundice and high ammonia content in his blood.

Dr. Mario Ravry cried with us. "I am so sorry, so very sorry," the chemotherapist whispered as he put his arms around both of us. "We will do all that we can to try and turn this thing around. Sometimes we can. But . . . it just doesn't look good."

It looked bad.

As days went by, it looked worse. Manget grew progressively weaker, yet his ministry grew greater.

One by one, he sent for our sons. Jeff came home from college for three days; the following weekend Tim and his lovely wife, Vicky, took Air Force leave and came home. Manget talked privately with each one of them, just as he had talked with Jon, our youngest who was completing his junior year of high school. "Through the years I have tried to teach you how to *live*," he told them, "and now God has given me the opportunity to teach you how to die." And he did.

Jon later said, "Mom, Dad can't lose. If he lives, he wins and we get to have him longer. If he dies, he will be with God, and that is even greater. Either way, he wins!" Manget had taught them well.

One month following gall bladder surgery Manget returned to the Georgia Baptist Medical Center. For six days his spirit struggled within him. I remember quite clearly the things he told me during his last conscious days:

"I am not afraid to die. I don't *want* to. I don't want to leave you. But I am not afraid."

Later he said, "It really is true. God does give 'dying grace'—it is *not* just words. It is real. I am ready."

He counseled me. "Whatever you do, don't be angry with God. I don't know why this is happening, but it is for good. You and I may never see or know why or what or where, but good will come."

"I love you and I don't want to leave you. . . ."

But he did.

After he had shared his faith anew with our sons; after he had told me all about finances and insurance and business matters which I had never handled before; after he told me how to divide some of his personal effects among the boys; after he spent his last days encouraging and comforting those who came to see him; after he settled spiritual matters with God, prepared perfectly to be reunited with his Creator and Savior, in the quietness of an early spring Saturday night, his struggling spirit was released silently and gently from the bondage of human flesh.

In the greatest hour of human need that I have ever known in my lifetime, God was there.

As the anguish of my broken heart seared my very soul, there was at the same time a strange, inexpressible *joy.* There was a peace that *does* transcend our understanding. I remember turning a short time later to my pastor, J. Hoffman Harris, and expressing aloud the one thought that had been going through my mind: "There was no 'sting.' It hurts, Hoffman, oh, how it hurts! But, *there is no sting!*"

In the time of grief and sorrow, through loving and caring friends, and in numerous surprising and unusual ways, truly, "the Word became flesh and dwelt among us." (John 1:14, RSV).

—Through a church community who gave flowers, foods, books, cards, visits, shared tears and cooperative hope, He was there.

—In the person of mission family, Foreign Mission Board staff, overseas calls and cables, personal presence; in the ministry of Dr. Charles Bryan, overseas vice-president, who came to assist in the funeral service, in their flesh—He was there.

Echoes from the past invaded my mourning with sudden and joyous consolation. A phone call came from our beloved former college professor, Dr. Arthur Walker, Jr., now serving as executive director-treasurer of the Education Commission of the Southern Baptist Convention. I knew how pleased Manget would have been that he cared enough to call. It helped to mend my shattered spirit just to talk with him. When he said, "I don't know what to say, but I just had to call," I learned a personal lesson. It isn't "what we say" in times of grief—it's just so important that we care enough to say *something*.

Another call from J. P. and Dottie Allen, formerly with the Radio and Television Commission of the Southern Baptist Convention in Fort Worth, was another reminder of past days and affected confidence in crisis. J. P. was the man who put Manget in touch with the first Baptist convert in Grenada and had later made return visits to the island, lending ministry and encouragement to us in the initial phases of our work there. His call from Golden Gate Baptist Theological Seminary where he was then teaching was like an arm reaching out in comforting confirmation of our missionary ministry and service.

When my heart was crying out, *It doesn't seem fair!*

He was only fifty years old! I received a beautiful letter from our friend, Jeannette Clift George. (Remember the pendant—the "hiding place"?) God used her spiritual wisdom to say to me through her correspondence, "God's infallible economy! I am awed by all that Manget completed in fifty years. In a time that has forgotten commitment, Manget illustrated it. That illustration has its price. God will swamp you with blessings—dear friendly soldier—and I will uphold you in prayer. God's grace is sufficient!"

Calls and letters continued to come. As the list grew, I basked in the comfort that God afforded me through flesh and blood. My faith was growing afresh and anew. God was there, just as He had promised. He would not leave me to grieve alone. He was dwelling with me, using people from our past as living reminders of His presence and His faithfulness in days gone by, assuring me that I was not in my valley alone. Those who had rejoiced with us so often in our rejoicing now wept with me in my weeping.

In death, Satan was defeated.

There is only one word that can adequately describe the events immediately following Manget's funeral: *victory*.

Our pastor wrote a moving tribute for the Briarlake Baptist Church newsletter. That item did not remain confined to the church publication. It was picked up and reprinted in its entirety in *The Daily Times* (Gainesville, Georgia). Most of the column, plus an additional tribute, appeared in *The Commission* of August 1983, our Foreign Mission Board news journal. I share it with you here.

HE DIED WELL

On one occassion John Wesley was asked the secret of Methodism. He responded by saying, "Our people die well." I have never seen this more eloquently done than a week ago when Manget Herrin, our missionary in residence, went to be with the Lord. Manget served fourteen years as missionary in British Guyana and Grenada. Prior to that he had served pastorates in Georgia and Alabama. He came back to the States less than a year ago to take a position with the Georgia Baptist Convention Stewardship Department, to give his youngest son stability in his last two years of high school and prepare him for college. In less than two months after arrival here, he learned that he had a malignancy. He was hopeful, took all the treatments gladly, did everything medical science prescribed, prayed earnestly, and wanted to live. In recent weeks the doctors confirmed what he knew within his own body—that he did not have long to live. As a true soldier of Jesus Christ, he accepted the will of his Commanding Officer without question. Oh, yes, he was human. He shed tears. He shared some very tender moments with me and Elaine as he talked about the reality of death and the end that would come soon, but he never questioned the will of God. He made his funeral arrangements. That in itself was a blessing to his family for this was the first time they had experienced the death of a family member. They knew exactly what he wanted. He assured them he did not want them to grieve nor to frequently visit the cemetery because he would not be there; he would be with the Lord.

A couple of hours before his death, the Lord gave him a foretaste of heaven as he was greeting loved ones on the other side. He quietly went to be with the Lord. He died as he lived, in quiet serene submission to the will of his Father.

As you would expect, Elaine taught her Sunday

School class yesterday, the Sunday following his death. She and Jon were joyful in worship, surrounded by friends.

On one occasion, Melanchthon was asked what was the greatest achievement of his life, and he answered, "Showing two boys the way they ought to go." There were many achievements in Manget's life, but one of the greatest was showing three sons the way they ought to go. They demonstrated that they understood his teachings as they stood by his bedside and watched life ebb away. They demonstrated it by the way they behaved in times of grief and sorrow. Tim, the oldest is serving in the armed forces in Tampa, Florida. It was on his strong arm that his mother walked into the sanctuary for the funeral service. He was dressed in his uniform, giving silent testimony of his father's love for his native country. Jeff followed. Jeff will graduate next week from Davidson College as an honor student, symbolizing again the love of truth that Manget had in his heart; that all men might come to know the truth that is in Jesus. Then there was Jon, tall, handsome and with a smile on his face. He has been closer to his father in recent years than the other two boys since they had left home. During this past year he and his father shared many close moments, and his father prepared Jon for his death and the difficult days to follow. Jon demonstrated a commitment to Jesus Christ and love for people that was so evident in his father's life.

Perhaps one of the most significant expressions was at the graveside when Forrest Lanier, vice-president of development at Shorter College, and who had led several lay teams to do mission work to help Manget in Grenada, was there and I asked him to lead the benediction. He said there was one there who could do it more eloquently than he. He called a beautiful Grenadian girl to his side. She had been brought to Athens by the Beech Haven Chruch. Some members who had gone to Grenada from that church had met her. She was born with a deformed leg which causes her to limp badly. The church brought her here and they have made plans for her to enter Scottish Rite Hospital in Atlanta next week for corrective surgery. As Forrest placed his arm around the lovely black girl, he asked if she would like to lead the benediction. With tears welling in her eyes, she shook her head negatively. She was overcome by emotion and could not speak. Then Forrest said that one word Manget used frequently was the word, "until," and he said, "let this word 'until' be the benediction." Then there was a dramatic pause and he said, "amen."

Yes, as I stood at that graveside thinking of the word "until," I looked into the grave where his ravaged body was being placed, and I thought, " *Until* Jesus comes, we shall not realize the meaning of our tears; *until* Jesus comes, we cannot know the fullness of salvation; *until* Jesus comes, we shall never know the quality and the fullness of Manget's life, *until* Jesus comes, we shall never know how far-reaching the gospel of Christ is." "Though he be dead, yet shall he live." Thank you, Lord, for his fifty years lived for you and for eternity to praise you. UNTIL . . .

—Dr. J. Hoffman Harris
Pastor
Briarlake Baptist Church Beacon
Decatur, Georgia

Less than two weeks after the funeral, I went to North Carolina for Jeff's graduation. Manget had so wanted to live to see Jeff graduate from college. Now I traveled to the graduation ceremonies without him.

There was only one way to face that and other difficult days that lay ahead. I would draw from the principles of living which Manget had taught me. I would continue to embrace the same mental attitudes that had guided us through those difficult months of illness and uncertainty.

Though my heart ached with an even greater sense of loss, and a certain emptiness threatened at moments to engulf me, I remembered: "Don't be angry with God . . . look for the good." I looked at my sister-in-law and dear friend (one and the same), Doris, seated beside me. Next to her was Manget's eldest brother. Harold had only recently recovered from surgery himself. How glad I was that they could join me! The day was beautiful. Gray morning skies that had threatened earlier to move the traditional outdoor ceremony inside had yielded to a bright blue morning. The graduates would not be disappointed. And that was good.

God's grace upheld me through the ceremony. When the president announced "Jeffrey Scott Herrin," supportive and sensitive students joined me in sustained applause. Through my tears, I looked up through the treetops into the clearing morning sky. "He did it," I whispered in my heart, "and with honors."

I was not alone.

So now I sit in "his chair," my feet curled up under me, the manuscript clutched in my hands. No, I will not write that chapter over. The outcome we had so longed for had not been ours. But the principles had not changed.

Had we not lived and operated under the precepts so outlined, we could not have faced—and triumphed—in the face of disappointment. And death.

There is still an abiding faith in God, confidence in medical achievements, strength from Christian love, power in the Word of God; and laughter still heals many wounds.

No. I would not change the manuscript.

But other things have changed.

I look at people differently.

I stopped at a traffic light behind a young family the other morning. I watched the young mother quarreling with two children in the backseat. Something within me wanted to jump out of my own car and run to their window and shout, "Don't! Please don't! Love your moments! Cherish your time together. You will not always have each other."

When I go into a cafeteria I often watch couples come in to eat. Sometimes it seems that I am the only one not "a couple." They sit there, all ages, sometimes arguing, more often silent, bored. My initial reaction is that of anger. The selfish, personal is first: *Why am I alone? Why do they still have each other?* God surely understands my frustrations and occasional questioning. That's why I love Him so—I can reveal to Him my very, very humanness and know that he *does* understand!

Then my mind quickly races to the tables around me, and I am obsessed with a desire to startle the fortunate couples out of their complacency. "Talk!" I want to order, "Mark your moments! They are gifts from God and good fortune in life, and there you sit, taking them for granted and throwing them away."

And I read the obituaries now.

My eyes scan the pages and I wonder why most of the deceased are seventy or eighty or ninety years old, and then I question again why my own loving husband only had fifty years. Why have so many survived so much, and why was he not healed?

But just as quickly as I ask the recurring question, I remember others who had even fewer years, and I am silenced. I rejoice that God chose to answer that question for me long before I asked it.

In 1980, Dr. Barrie White, President of Regent's Park College at Oxford, came to Grenada for a rest-vacation. He was accompanied by his wife, Margaret. Before they returned to England, they visited our church and we became friends. They invited us to dinner, and we shared a common faith and similar concerns.

On their final day there, Margaret visited in my women's Sunday School class. She sat quietly as the women animatedly discussed some firsthand knowledge of God's miraculous healing in the lives of various individuals. At the conclusion of the lesson, Margaret offered her own contribution.

"A speaker at our women's group recently shared her own experience of healing," Margaret told us. "She related how she had been stricken with cancer, had prayed earnestly, and had been completely cured. She went on to say that sometime later her husband was diagnosed with the same dread disease. Again they prayed and believed God. Her husband died."

Mrs. White said that the speaker was questioned later, "Can you explain why you think God healed you and did not heal your husband?"

"Oh, you don't understand. He *was* healed. You see, my healing is only temporary. I have been sick since and will surely be sick again. But my husband? He received the *perfect healing*. He will never suffer or be sick again."

Margaret White shared that moving and thought-provoking account seated in a circle of lovely black West Indian women on the veranda of our small mission church three years ago. I was deeply touched by the beauty of another Christian's interpretation and acceptance of one of life's mysteries. Little did I know that the story would return to minister to me. Yet, less than three years later, after watching one who was "so alive" debilitate and suffer, I could calm my broken heart and bereaved soul with the assurance that my loving husband had received "perfect healing."

In that initial healing process for my own spirit and that of our family, another friend shared a powerful reminder that even in the very moments of death, we are not alone. The poet so masterfully penned it, that even as we read the verse incribed in lovely calligraphy art, we smiled through tears of affirmative joy.

Perspective

I am standing on the seashore.
  A ship spreads her sails to the morning
breeze, and starts for the ocean.
  I stand watching her until she fades
on the horizon.
  And someone at my side says,
            "She is gone!"
Gone where? The loss of sight is
  in ME, not in HER.
At that moment when someone says,
            "She is gone,"
There are others who are watching her coming. Other
voices take up the glad shout, - - - - - "Here she comes!"
            And that is dying.
                        —Henry Scott Holland

My house is large and the rooms are uncomfortably silent. Days come and go, and in them God presents new opportunities and challenges for ministry in unusual and different ways.

Never before have I been so humanly "alone."

Yet, in the quietness of each new day, God's Word comforts me with the assurance that He has not left me; He has not forsaken me. The past has proved it, the present promises me, and the future assures me: I am . . . *never alone.*

Notes

1. Paul Tournier, *Guilt and Grace* (New York: Harper and Row, 1962), p. 45.

2. Norman Cousins, *Anatomy of an Illness* (New York: Bantam, 1981), pp. 39-40.